O LITTLE TOWN

O LITTLE TOWN

*Hymn tunes
and the places that inspired them*

Mark Browse

Copyright © Mark Browse 2015

All rights reserved

ISBN 978-1-326-29701-5

Contents

Introduction 1

A short history of English hymns 7

Crimond 19

Innsbruck 29

Repton 39

Jerusalem 55

Thaxted 63

Abbot's Leigh 73

Cwm Rhondda 83

Down Ampney 95

Kingsfold 105

Monks Gate 121

Forest Green 135

Everywhere else 145

Acknowledgements 153

Picture credits 155

Works consulted 157

Index 163

Introduction

ONE SONG TO THE TUNE OF ANOTHER

Index of Tunes from the first edition of *Hymns Ancient & Modern* (1861)

INTRODUCTION

One song to the tune of another

EVERYONE KNOWS AT LEAST SOME HYMNS. Even if you are not a church-goer you will almost certainly be familiar with some of the more famous ones. Christmas songs like *While shepherds watched their flocks by night* and *O little town of Bethlehem* are hymns, even though we call them carols. You might also remember some Easter hymns like *There is a green hill far away*; and as schoolchildren many of us sang old favourites like *Onward, Christian soldiers* and *To be a pilgrim*. Hymns are part of our shared culture. Even the British National Anthem, *God Save the Queen*, is a hymn.

Of course, if you do attend church from time to time you will probably know a great many more hymns. It is even possible that you enjoy singing them. It has to be admitted that there are some pretty awful hymns, but there are many excellent ones that can stir the spirit or calm the troubled soul.

As with all songs, the power of a good hymn lies in the perfect marriage of words and music. The popularity of *Dear Lord and Father of mankind* or *For all the saints* comes from their tunes at least as much as their text. What you may not know, however, even if you are a regular church-goer, is that hymn-tunes have NAMES.

Let me explain. Most other types of song are a complete fusion of words and music, and it would be nonsense to give the tune one title and the words another. The name of the tune for *Yesterday* is *Yesterday*; the name of the tune for *You'll never walk alone* is *You'll never walk alone*; the name of the tune for *My old man's a dustman* is *My old man's a dustman*; and so on. It is ridiculous to think of the words and the music as two separate entities. Radio 4's *I'm Sorry I Haven't a Clue* gets a lot of comic mileage out of this fact:

O LITTLE TOWN

'We're going to play now a rather complicated game called *One Song To The Tune Of Another*, which may need some explanation. In it, teams, we take a song, or tune, and remove the lyrics, or words, from the tune, or song, and then, and this explains why we call it *One Song to the Tune of Another*, we take the lyrics, or words, away from another tune, or song, and get you to sing the words with the tune from the first song, without the lyrics, but with the music. And if this were not challenge enough, teams, accompaniment will be provided by Colin Sell at the piano...'[1]

Hymn-singers play this 'rather complicated game' all the time. Many hymns can be sung to more than one different tune. John Newton's well-known hymn *Glorious things of thee are spoken* fits a wonderful melody by Cyril Taylor, but also has a long history of being sung to a tune by Haydn. And both these tunes can be used for different words: the Haydn one is often used for *Praise the Lord, ye heavens adore him*, while Taylor's tune has been borrowed for various texts, despite having been written originally for Newton's words.

Many hymns, of course, are inextricably tied to their tunes. For instance, it would be absurd, and possibly illegal, to sing the National Anthem to any other tune; and it is difficult to imagine *O come all ye faithful* or *Onward, Christian soldiers* being sung to anything but their well-known melodies. But not all the old traditional hymns are as old or as traditional as you might think, or as closely bound to their familiar tunes; and many of them have in the past been sung to completely different ones. *While shepherds watched* has been set to several different tunes, including *On Ilkla Moor baht 'at*. (This is sometimes claimed as the national anthem of Yorkshire, but it was originally meant to be a hymn-tune.)

The upshot of all this infidelity between words and music is that editors of hymn-books need to be able to refer to the TUNES without having

---

[1] BBC Radio 4, May 1995. Quoted by permission.

4

to mention the *words* of a hymn. You can't airily talk of the tune for *Glorious things of thee are spoken* without being specific: do you mean the Haydn tune or the Taylor tune? To get round this problem, all hymn-tunes are given a NAME.

These tune-names do occasionally refer to the words that go with them. John Goss's noble tune for *Praise, my soul, the King of Heaven* is called PRAISE MY SOUL; while one of the two well-known tunes for *All things bright and beautiful* is actually called ALL THINGS BRIGHT AND BEAUTIFUL. But in most cases the name of the tune gives no clue about which words it is intended for. This is even true for hymns that are virtually only ever sung to one tune. For example, the tune for *Onward, Christian soldiers* is called ST GERTRUDE, and the tune for *Come down, O Love divine* is called DOWN AMPNEY.

Most hymn-books are printed in at least two different versions: an edition with only the words (for the congregation) and an edition which prints the music as well (for the choir and organist). The music edition will usually have an index of tunes, listing all the melodies printed in the book, with their tune-name. Here is a hymn-book from my shelves: it is a copy of the 1933 edition of *The English Hymnal*. Opening the ALPHABETICAL INDEX OF TUNES at random at the letter F, I find the first few entries are as follows:

FALKLAND	FFIGYSBREN
FARLEY CASTLE	FIRST MODE MELODY
FARMBOROUGH	FITZWILLIAM
FARNABY	FOLKINGHAM
FARNHAM	FOR ALL THE SAINTS
FARRANT	FOREST GREEN

What strikes me about this list, and indeed about the whole ALPHABETICAL INDEX OF TUNES of this and other hymn-books, is that many of the tune-names are also place-names. If I'd started at the letter A I might have included Aberdeen, Aberystwyth and Abbot's Leigh; from the letter B I could have mentioned Bangor, Bedford and Belgrave; and so on all the way to Wigton and Yorkshire. I have not done a detailed statistical study, but I would guess that at least a quarter of hymn-tunes have names that are taken from a city, town, country or other geographical entity.

This set me thinking. Why do hymn-tunes get named after places so often? And when they do, what is the connection between the tune and the place?

The answer to those questions is the subject-matter of this book. To find the connection we are going to embark on a journey—a journey where our guide is not a map or even a satnav, but a hymn-book. It is a journey that will take us to some unexpected places and reveal some surprising links.

❖

But before we set off, let's have a quick history lesson.

Chapter 1

A SHORT HISTORY OF ENGLISH HYMNS

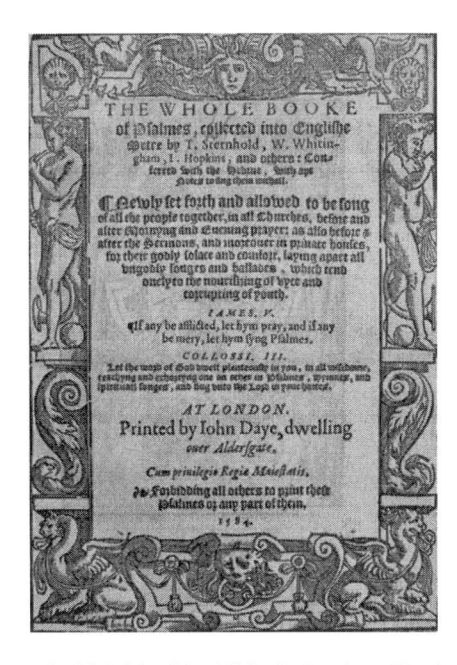

Sternhold & Hopkins' *Whole Booke of Psalmes*

A short history of English hymns

And why they are named after places

THERE HAVE PROBABLY BEEN HYMNS OF SOME KIND since the dawn of humanity. Music and sacred ritual are among the things that are found in every human culture, and it is not surprising to find them combined in holy songs. In the Old Testament there are many such songs, most notably the collection of 150 lyrics which we know as the Book of Psalms. In the early Christian era the Psalms continued to be the main source of texts for religious singing; to these were added some lyrics from the New Testament like the *Magnificat* ('My soul doth magnify the Lord') and the *Nunc Dimittis* ('Lord, now lettest thou thy servant depart in peace'), and a number of Latin hymns written in the fourth, fifth and sixth centuries: these include the *Te Deum* ('We praise thee O God') as well as some poems that have become well-known as hymns in their English translations, like *Pange Lingua* ('Sing, my tongue, the glorious battle'). Many of these Latin verses are ascribed to St Ambrose: there is a legend that the *Te Deum* was improvised by Ambrose and St Augustine at the latter's baptism.

Until the Reformation, these Latin hymns and the Biblical texts would have been the only songs heard in church. Indeed, the whole of the church service would have been in Latin, and the vast majority of the congregation would not have had a clue about what was going on. The tradition of ringing a bell at the elevation of the Host—still done in Roman Catholic churches and at the high end of Anglican worship—originated as a way of alerting the congregation to the fact that something significant was happening: a fact that they would otherwise have missed because all the talking and singing was in a language they didn't understand. It is near this point in the service that the priest says '*hoc est corpus meum*—this is my body—and perhaps because of the ringing of the bell people noticed this phrase with its funny foreign words. When people wanted to make fun of the Papists these were the words that they seized on, but because they had misheard them *hoc est corpus* became *hocus pocus*, a mock-magical formula representing meaningless ritual.

The emergence of the Church of England

In 1534 Henry VIII finally broke away from the Roman Catholic Church, appointing himself 'the only supreme head on earth of the Church of England'. This was not quite the same thing as the Reformation, which was a movement begun on the Continent questioning the teachings and practices of the Catholic Church. Henry did not recognise the power of the Pope, but in most other respects he was still Catholic, not Protestant. When he died in 1547 church services were still being held mostly in Latin. There were English translations of the Bible, but this was a controversial development, and at the end of Henry's reign the only version permitted was the Great Bible compiled by Miles Coverdale. It was called 'Great' because it was physically huge. This made it ideal for use in churches, but also had the advantage (as Henry saw it) that ordinary people could not afford it. He was not happy about the idea that the Word of God would be bandied about freely by commoners.

During the reign of Henry's successor Edward VI the church became decidedly Protestant, and services were held in English. Queen Mary, a Catholic, put things back to how they were before Henry VIII, with the Pope in charge of the Church, and services in Latin once more, hocus pocus and all.

When Elizabeth I came to the throne, the Church of England again spurned Rome and went back to using English. This meant that the congregation could follow what was happening, and even take part in it. It is really from this time that we can start talking about English hymn-singing.

Come before his presence with a song

In those early days it was thought that the only songs suitable for singing in church were the Psalms. These were considered to be the word of God, while anything else, however lofty its intentions, would merely be the word of Man, and hence an unworthy way to praise the Almighty. This idea had been imported from the Continent by English Protestants who had taken refuge in Geneva and elsewhere, in the years when questioning the church of Rome was a capital offence. Not all the European Protestants held this narrow view: in Germany, Martin Luther himself wrote a number of hymns and seemed happy for them to be sung alongside the divinely inspired Psalms. Many of Luther's hymns continue to be sung today, the most famous being *A safe stronghold our God is still*, sung to the tune EIN' FESTE BURG (which may also have been composed by Luther).

But in Tudor England only the Psalms would do.

Whatever the theological arguments behind this ruling, it caused a musical problem. To see why, have a look at this psalm:

> O be ioyfull in the Lorde (all ye landes) serue the Lorde with gladnes, and come before hys presence with a songe.
> Be ye sure, that the Lorde he is God: It is he that hath made vs, and not we oure selues: we are his people, and the shepe of his pasture.
> O go youre waye into hys gates with thanckesgeuyng, and into his courtes wyth prayse: be thankfull vnto hym, and speake good of hys name.
> For the Lorde is gracyous, hys mercy is euerlastynge, and his treuth endureth from generacion to generacion.

This is Psalm 100 as it appears in the Great Bible. I have given it in its original spelling partly for authenticity and partly because I think it has a certain charm: I particularly like 'thanckesgeuyng'. In modern spelling, as it appears in current editions of the Book of Common Prayer, it goes as follows:

O LITTLE TOWN

> O be joyful in the Lord, all ye lands: serve the Lord with gladness, and come before his presence with a song.
> Be ye sure that the Lord he is God: it is he that hath made us, and not we ourselves; we are his people, and the sheep of his pasture.
> O go your way into his gates with thanksgiving, and into his courts with praise: be thankful unto him, and speak good of his Name.
> For the Lord is gracious, his mercy is everlasting: and his truth endureth from generation to generation.

The language is beautiful: the Prayer Book is rightly considered to be one of the monuments of English literature. The trouble is it does not look very much like a song.

Most songs, and virtually all hymns, have some kind of metre—that is, a regular rhythm that is repeated to create a pattern. The most common pattern, used in countless songs, poems, hymns, doggerel and nursery rhymes, is—appropriately—known as Common Metre (or sometimes Common Measure). It consists of four lines: the first and third have eight syllables, while the second and fourth have six. Here's an example:

> *O God, our help in ages past,*
> *Our hope for years to come,*
> *Our shelter from the stormy blast,*
> *And our eternal home.*

And here's another with the same basic rhythmic pattern (though the syllable-count is not quite as strict):

> *Mary had a little lamb,*
> *Its fleece was white as snow,*
> *And everywhere that Mary went*
> *The lamb was sure to go.*

As well as Common Metre there are many other patterns that have been used in songs and hymns; but they all have *some* kind of metre. Anything that is sung by a congregation, or a classroom, or a group of people down the pub, or a crowd of football fans, will have some sort of regular rhythmic organisation.

Songs nearly always have rhyme, too. Not all poetry rhymes, of course, but songs almost always do; though in the case of folk-music and popular songs the rhymes often are only approximate. I can think of only one hymn that doesn't rhyme: *O come all ye faithful*; and the words of that are so familiar that it doesn't seem to matter.

For congregational, community singing, there is no doubt that what works best is a song with regular metre and rhyme.

If we look back at Psalm 100 we find it has none of these things, in the Prayer Book translation. Each verse is a different length and rhythm, and there are no rhymes at all. How are you supposed to sing this?

Well, it is of course possible to set words like this to music. One approach would be to vary the melodic line to fit the words, so instead of a song with patterns that are repeated in each verse you get a 'through-composed' piece where the music reflects the words and adapts itself to them, rather than simply being a vehicle for proclaiming them. There are many examples of psalms being set to music in this way; indeed, I have composed a setting of Psalm 100 myself. But these are usually only suitable for trained choirs who have had a chance to practise: they do not suit congregational singing.

Another way of singing psalms straight out of the Prayer Book is to *chant* them. Anglican chant, as it is still practised in churches today, emerged from medieval plainchant. It uses a simple melody, usually harmonised in four parts. To make the tune fit the irregular lines of the psalm, some of the notes are designated 'chanting notes', which means that a varying number of syllables are sung to these notes, depending on how many have to be fitted in. So in the beginning of Psalm 100 the words 'O be joyful in the Lord' would all be on one chord, as would 'serve the Lord with gladness, and come before his...'. Something like this:

O Little Town

[Musical notation: "O be joyful in the Lord all ye lands: serve the Lord with gladness, and come before his pre-sence with a song."]

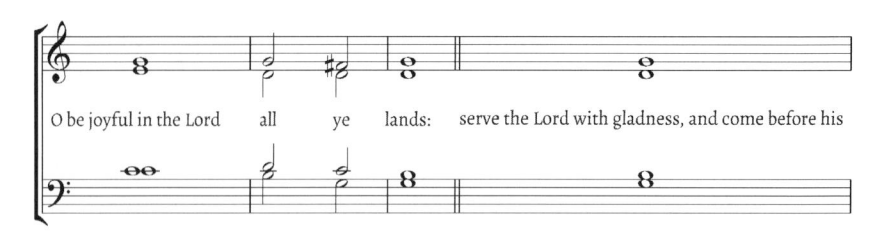

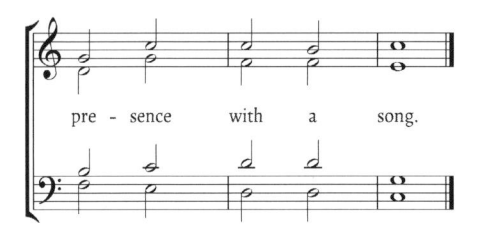

When done well, Anglican chant can be very beautiful. But once again it is not something that congregations can easily do without practice.

Sing to the Lord with cheerful voice

So the Elizabethan church had a problem. On the one hand only the Psalms were considered suitable for singing in services: on the other, they were written in a way which was not very song-like.

The solution, again borrowed from European Protestants, was to do a new translation of the Psalms which did have regular rhythm and rhyme. These are known as *metrical psalms*. Here is what became of Psalm 100:

> *All people that on earth do dwell,*
> *Sing to the Lord with cheerful voice,*
> *Him serve with fear, his praise forth tell,*
> *Come ye before him and rejoice.*

This version of the psalm was probably written by William Kethe and was first published in Geneva in 1561. It is still familiar today, as is its tune, which in modern hymn-books is called the OLD HUNDREDTH.

The first English hymnal?

The first book to provide metrical versions in English of all 150 of the Psalms was *The Whole Book of Psalms*, compiled by Thomas Sternhold (1500–1549) and John Hopkins (1520–1570) and published in 1562 by John Day. This book is sometimes referred to as *Day's Psalter*, and sometimes known simply as 'Sternhold & Hopkins'. As well as being one of the first English hymn-books, it is also arguably the most successful: it was in constant use for nearly three centuries, and even when rival publications came out it was regarded with reverence and became known as the 'Old Version'. There had been collections of metrical psalms before Sternhold and Hopkins: Coverdale (the translator of the Great Bible) had brought one out in 1539, rather charmingly called *Goostly Psalms* (goostly or ghostly meaning 'spiritual'); however, this was not a complete collection of the Psalms, and in any case it was suppressed by Henry VIII.

The first edition of *Day's Psalter* had sixty-five tunes. There are 150 Psalms, so some of them had to share a tune: the origin of 'One Song to the Tune of Another'. Those psalms that did not have their own tune had a suggestion as to which other psalm's tune would be suitable: for example, next to Psalm 99 is the instruction 'Sing this as the 77. Psalme'.

The origin of tune names

In 1592, thirty years after Sternhold and Hopkins, Thomas Este (1540–1608) brought out another metrical psalter, which included tunes by some of the most distinguished composers of the day, such as John Dowland (1563?–1626). Este's book includes a sort of musical index showing the new tunes that were making their first appearance, and which psalms are suitable for them. This index also shows four tunes that are identified by a place-name: GLASSENBURY TUNE, KENTISH TUNE, SUFFOLK TUNE and CHESHIRE TUNE. This is the origin of the practice of giving hymn-tunes names that come from places.

In 1621 another important book was published, the *Psalter* by Thomas Ravenscroft (1591–16??). The tune index of Ravenscroft's book continues and extends Este's association of tunes with places: all the tunes listed are given the name of a city, town, cathedral, school or chapel where the tunes are commonly sung.

As an example, let's look at Psalm 23. In the Prayer Book it runs as follows:

> The Lord is my shepherd: therefore can I lack nothing.
> He shall feed me in a green pasture: and lead me forth beside the waters of comfort.

In the metrical version from Ravenscroft's Psalter it goes like this:

> *The Lord is onely my support,*
> *And he that doth me feede:*
> *How can I then lacke any thing,*
> *Whereof I stand in need?*
>
> *He doth me fold in coates most safe,*
> *The tender grasse fast by:*
> *And after drives me to the streames,*
> *Which run most pleasantly.*

The melody to which this is set is identified by Ravenscroft as being a WINCHESTER TUNE, meaning that it was commonly used there. In modern hymn-books this tune is called WINCHESTER OLD, and is now the most usual tune for *While shepherds watched their flocks by night*.

From then on the practice of identifying hymn-tunes with places became widespread. At the same time, it gradually became acceptable for devotional poems other than the Psalms to be included in hymn-books, thereby greatly increasing the number of texts for which tunes were needed. In the century after Este and Ravenscroft, writers such as Isaac Watts and John and Charles Wesley produced many lyrics that are still in use today, including *When I survey the wondrous cross* and *Hark the herald angels sing*. Wesley and his fellow Methodists placed hymn-singing at the centre of worship, and greatly enriched the repertoire of both words and music.

As the example below from one of John Wesley's collections shows, it was now usual to associate hymn-tunes with places. This melody, which Wesley calls BROMSWICK TUNE, is still sung today, usually to the hymn *O worship the King, all glorious above*. Modern hymn-books call this tune HANOVER; Bromswick or Brunswick (or Braunschweig to give it its modern spelling) is not far from Hannover in Germany, from which presumably the tune comes.

BROMSWICK TUNE, from John Wesley's
Foundery Collection

O LITTLE TOWN

The eighteenth and nineteenth centuries produced a cornucopia of hymn-words and hymn-tunes. In 1861 appeared the first edition of *Hymns Ancient & Modern*, the book which did for the late Victorian period what Sternhold and Hopkins had done for the Elizabethans. A glance at the Index of Tunes from this book shows that the great wealth of hymn-tunes now available meant that they could not all be named after places, and some much more fanciful titles were being used, like VEXILLA REGIS and WAR; nevertheless, place-names were still one of the most common sources for hymn-tune names: BEDFORD and BRISTOL; CHESHIRE and CHICHESTER; DURHAM and DUNDEE; WESTMINSTER, WINCHESTER and WINDSOR.

Hymns Ancient & Modern was not, of course, the last word in hymn-books: there have been many important publications since then, and indeed many new editions of *A&M* itself. Hymn-tunes continue to be written and given titles that are not simply the first line of the hymn for which they are intended. And place-names continue to be a major source of names for hymn-tunes.

In this book I explore the relationship between the tune and the place for a handful of hymns. This is not meant to be a scholarly work, or even remotely comprehensive. It is certainly not a work of reference. I have chosen tunes that are reasonably familiar, tunes that I like, and tunes that have a bit of a story behind them. Some of these stories I tell in detail, allowing myself to go off piste from time to time; for others, I give the briefest summary.

❖

THE TITLE OF THIS CHAPTER was *A short history of English hymns*, but it would have been better to say 'hymns in English': for the hymns and tunes we are about to explore are by no means all from England. Our first port of call is in Aberdeenshire, in Scotland.

Chapter 2

CRIMOND

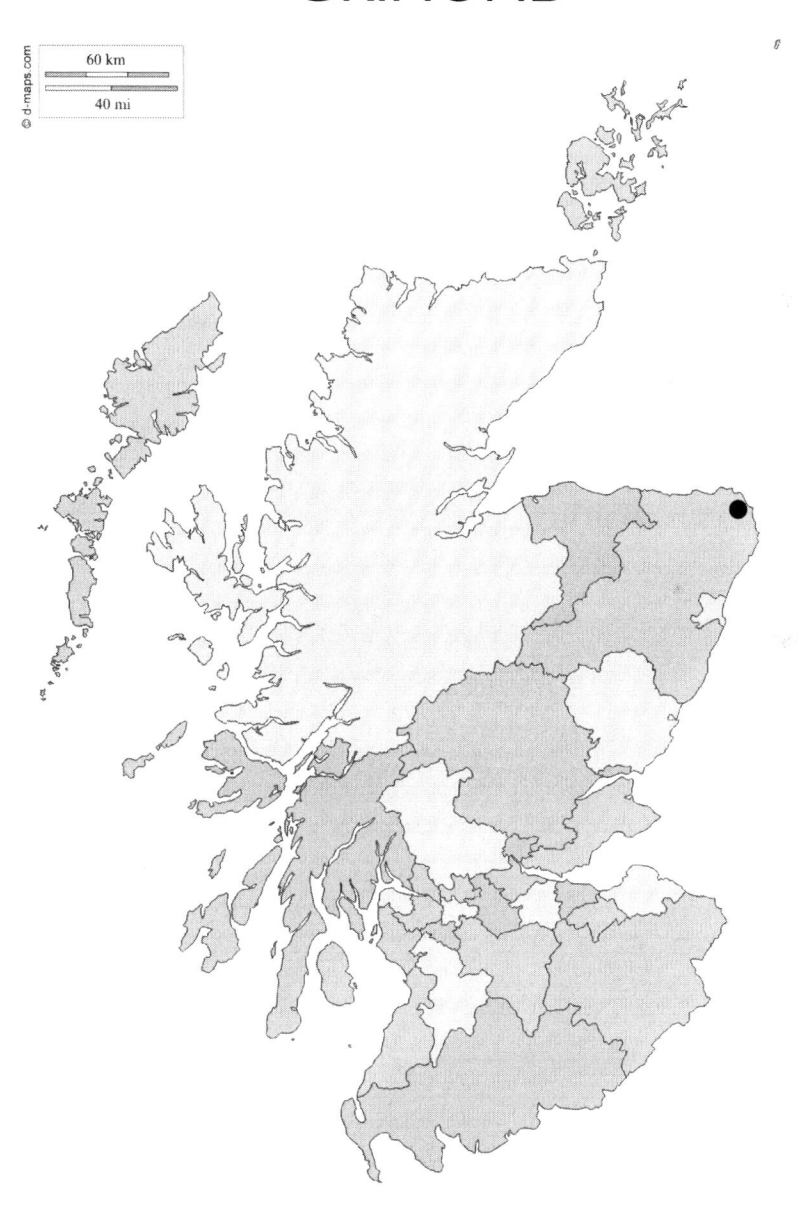

CRIMOND

The Lord's my shepherd

The Lord's my Shep-herd, I'll not want; he makes me down to lie

DAVID GRANT 1833-1893
OR JESSIE IRVINE 1836-1887

CRIMOND IS A VILLAGE about thirty miles from Aberdeen, on the road between Peterhead and Fraserburgh. The name of the village was originally Creichmont, which seems to come from a Gaelic name meaning 'cattle-moor'. There are certainly cattle—and sheep—in the surrounding countryside, which is full of green pastures; it is low-lying land, sloping gently down towards the sea. The houses are mostly modest and grey, occasionally with a hint of brown. Here and there the landscape in this area is punctuated by industrial buildings: this is North Sea oil country.

The clock on Crimond church

O LITTLE TOWN

The church in Crimond was built in 1812; it is a handsome building with a clock bearing the warning THE HOUR'S COMING. Apart from this it seems like a perfectly ordinary clock; but if you look closely you will see that there is an extra notch between the XI and the XII, so that each hour as measured by this clock has sixty-one minutes. In 1948 the clock was repaired and the face was repainted, with the hour divided into a more conventional number; but the locals objected and their extra minute was restored to them.

Like the clock, there is something stubbornly odd about the history of the hymn-tune CRIMOND—something you can't quite get hold of, something slightly misleading. It is one of the tunes commonly sung to *The Lord's my shepherd* (the other being BROTHER JAMES'S AIR). The connection between these words and this tune is so strong that you would be forgiven for thinking that they have always gone together. However, you would be wrong.

The unwanted shepherd?

The words of *The Lord's my shepherd* are a metrical version of Psalm 23, first published in *The Scottish Psalter* of 1650. This psalm, with its comforting imagery, is probably one of the best-loved in the book, so it is not surprising that there are several different metrical versions. We have already met the one that was included in Ravenscroft's *Psalter* of 1621, sung to WINCHESTER OLD—better known today as the tune to *While shepherds watched*. Another metrical version of Psalm 23, *The King of love my shepherd is*, was written by Sir Henry Williams Baker (1821-1877) and published in *Hymns Ancient & Modern* in 1868, set to the tune DOMINUS REGIT ME, specially composed for it by J B Dykes.

The version of the psalm that begins *The Lord's my shepherd* is enduringly popular, but it suffers from some difficulties. Like many hymns, it is in Common Metre: that is to say, there are four lines to each verse, alternating eight syllables and six syllables. Because of the natural rhythms of the English language, there is a tendency to pause longer after the six-syllable lines than after the eight-syllable ones. The trouble is, the meaning of the words in *The Lord's my shepherd* doesn't lend itself to this metrical pattern. If you were reading the first verse as poetry, trying to get across the sense of the words, you would probably do something like this:

> *The Lord's my shepherd,*
> *I'll not want.*
> *He makes me down to lie in pastures green;*
> *He leadeth me the quiet waters by.*

This is how it looks on the page:

> *The Lord's my shepherd, I'll not want.*
> *He makes me down to lie*
> *In pastures green; he leadeth me*
> *The quiet waters by.*

So there is an unnatural gap between the second and third lines, and another one between the third and the fourth; while there is not *enough* of a gap in the middle of the first line, with the result that it sounds as if the Lord is an unwanted shepherd. You can make it work as spoken poetry, but as soon as you set it to a tune that the congregation will want to sing, you mangle the meaning.

A postwar Royal Wedding

In 1947 our present Queen, then Princess Elizabeth, married Philip Mountbatten in Westminster Abbey. It was a suitably glittering occasion, a chance for some colour and splendour just two years after the end of the war. The guest list included most of the royalty of Europe, though there were some notable absences, including the Duke of Windsor (the former Edward VIII, who was not invited) and Prince Philip's own sisters (who were considered too German). The music for the service included a fanfare specially composed by Sir Arnold Bax, the Master of the King's Music; and the hymns were *Praise, my soul, the King of Heaven* (to the disappointingly-named tune PRAISE MY SOUL), and *The Lord's my shepherd*, to CRIMOND.

Nowadays CRIMOND is automatically associated with those words, but in fact the Royal Wedding was one of the earliest public occasions on which these words and this tune were paired up. When the tune was first published, in 1872, it was given the following text:

Thou art the Way, the Truth, the Life:
grant us that way to know,
that truth to keep, that life to win,
whose joys eternal flow.

This is the last verse of a hymn by G W Doane, which begins 'Thou art the Way, to thee alone from sin and death we flee'.

The idea of setting CRIMOND to *The Lord's my shepherd* seems to have come from one John McEwan, a choirmaster from Glasgow who was also a member of the Glasgow Orpheus Choir. In 1936 that choir performed *The Lord's my shepherd* to CRIMOND in the Queen's Hall in London, under their conductor Hugh Roberton. Later they made a recording of the hymn, and this did much to fix the connection between text and tune in the mind of the public. The recording is painfully slow by modern standards, and it is notable that the Orpheus Choir makes no attempt to iron out the mismatch between metre and meaning that I referred to above: there is a blatant breath between 'lie' and 'in pastures green' which would no doubt cause much distress to officers of the Royal School of Church Music.

Thanks to the Glasgow Orpheus Choir and the Royal Wedding of 1947—and also the Silver Wedding of George VI and Queen Elizabeth in 1948—British hymn-singers began to associate the metrical version of

Psalm 23 with CRIMOND. This combination of words and music went on to become a staple of non-royal weddings, and it is now difficult to imagine CRIMOND being sung to any other hymn.

The origins of CRIMOND

Around the year 1859 a journalist from Aberdeen called William Carnie began to collect Scottish hymns and publish them in leaflet form. In 1872 he gathered these together into a book called *The Northern Psalter*. This book became extremely successful, and tens of thousands of copies were sold. This was the first hymn-book to feature CRIMOND, which the earliest editions attributed to David Grant (1833-1893).

Crimond Parish Church

Grant was a tobacconist from Aberdeen. As well as CRIMOND, *The Northern Psalter* included another tune by him, named RALEIGH in honour of Sir Walter Raleigh, who introduced tobacco to Britain. Grant was one of a group of people who worked with William Carnie on collecting and classifying Scottish hymns—mostly metrical settings of the Psalms. Other members of the group included Robert Cooper, who was the precentor (director of music) in Peterhead, and William Clubb, a saddler who was also precentor at the church in Crimond. It was Cooper who suggested the name CRIMOND for Grant's tune, presumably in honour of Clubb.

A rival claim

For many years David Grant was credited as the composer of CRIMOND, and there was no suggestion that he might not be. By 1908, when William Carnie died, *The Northern Psalter* had sold over 70,000 copies, all of them stating that Grant had written the tune. This went unchallenged until the 1940s, and was still assumed to be true at the time of the Queen's wedding in 1947. But around that time a letter came to light which cast doubt on this hitherto universally accepted attribution.

The letter in question had been written in 1911 by Anna Barbara Irvine, daughter of the Revd Alexander Irvine, who was minister of Crimond church from 1855; it was addressed to the Revd Robert Monteith, who was himself minister at Crimond from 1909. In this letter, Anna states that the tune had in fact been composed by her sister, Jessie Seymour Irvine, who had died in 1887, and that David Grant's contribution had simply been that he provided the harmony.

In 1947 this letter came to the attention of the Revd Dr Millar Patrick, who published an article in the *Bulletin of the Hymn Society* the following year claiming that Jessie Irvine was in fact the composer of CRIMOND. Monteith also went into print supporting this claim: in 1948 he wrote to *The Scotsman* mentioning the letter he had received from Jessie

Irvine's sister, which he said was in response to an enquiry by the Revd Dr Kemp, minister of the parish of Deer.

What Monteith did not mention in his correspondence in *The Scotsman* was that in 1911, shortly after Anna Irvine had written to him, he had received a letter from George Riddell (another of William Carnie's collaborators on *The Northern Psalter*) and William Clubb, the precentor of Crimond at the time the tune was written. They claimed that Anna had been mistaken when she stated that Jessie had composed CRIMOND. It was true, they said, that she had written a tune that was harmonised by David Grant: but this tune was one called BALLANTINE, the manuscript of which was in the possession of Clubb. Riddell and Clubb were of the opinion that Anna had muddled up the two tunes, perhaps because the name Ballantine had some unfortunate associations for her.

The controversy endures

So who really did write CRIMOND? David Grant was credited as the composer for many years without anyone raising a doubt. If Jessie Irvine had indeed written the tune, there was plenty of time before 1947 for her—or a member of her family—to have raised an objection. Yet we are still left with a little uneasiness, like an extra minute between 11 o'clock and 12 o'clock. For instance, if Grant was the composer, why was the tune called CRIMOND? To say it was in honour of his associate William Clubb is a little tenuous; but if Jessie Irvine wrote it, the name is perfectly understandable. And why should we totally discredit Anna Irvine's letter?

Whatever the truth, there is a muddle over CRIMOND, with some sources supporting Grant and others Irvine. Grabbing a couple of fairly recent hymn-books from my shelf, I find that *Common Praise* (2000) says the tune is by David Grant, while *The New English Hymnal* (1986) attributes it to Jessie Irvine. The Wikipedia entry for Crimond says it is by Irvine, as does the article in Hymnary.org; on the other hand the *Canterbury Dictionary of Hymnology* tentatively suggests that the Grantists are correct, while admitting that 'the matter is still in some doubt.'

O Little Town

At the back of the church in Crimond are four arched windows commemorating the church's association with the hymn-tune. These were installed in memory of the Revd James E Lyall, who was minister from 1993–2002. They are beautifully engraved with part of the tune and with images representing the Good Shepherd. The first of these windows bears the following inscription:

> The 23rd Psalm: Crimond tune composed by Jessie Seymour Irvine 1836 – 87.

It is clear that the people of Crimond are in no doubt about who was the true composer of the tune.

❖

Our next stop is many hundreds of miles away, in an Austrian city whose beauty inspired a poignant love-song.

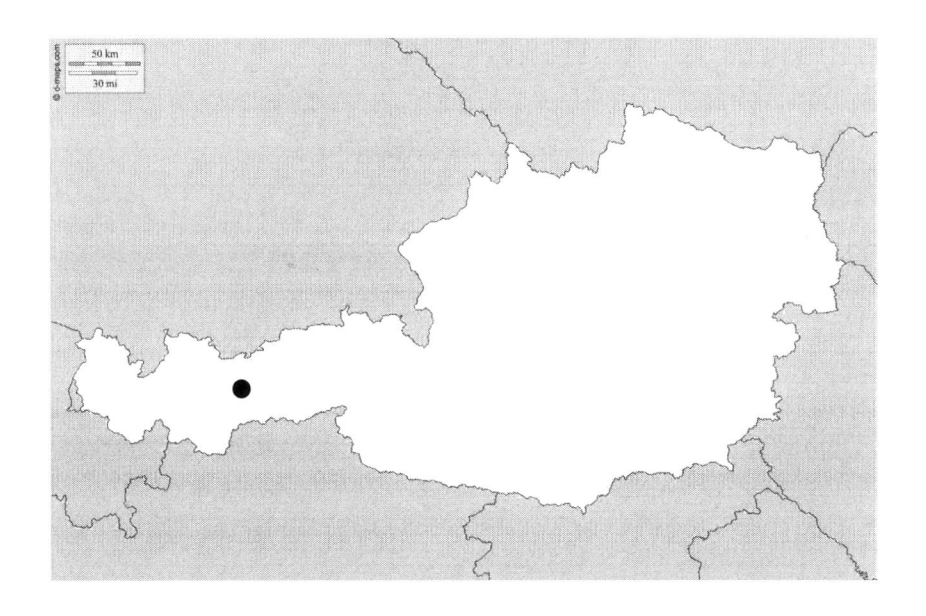

Chapter 3
INNSBRUCK

INNSBRUCK

The duteous day now closeth

The dut-eous day now clos-eth, each flower and tree re-pos-eth,

HEINRICH ISAAC 1450-1517

I T IS EARLY JANUARY, and Innsbruck is all dressed up in its Christmas finery. At any time of year its medieval centre would probably look like something from a Christmas card, with its sinuous streets and cobbled courtyards; and the addition of a generous layer of snow on the roofs completes the effect. Large dolls are hung from the walls of some of the older buildings, representing fairytale characters. Some of them are familiar, such as Little Red Riding-Hood; others are less so, like *der Hase und der Igel* (a tall thin hare in a smart jacket, and a hedgehog in a check shirt—from a story by the Brothers Grimm). Christmas lights are strung across the streets, the shops are decorated with stars and angels, and many delicately carved Nativity scenes are on display.

The Hare and the Hedgehog in Innsbruck

O Little Town

Innsbruck is the capital of the Austrian region of Tyrol. The city is named after the River Inn, which flows through the Alps from its source in Switzerland and through Austria until it meets the Danube in Bavaria. The second syllable of Innsbruck does not mean 'brook' (which in German is *Bach*): it is a variant of *Brücke*, which means 'bridge'. As we shall see, the hymn-tune called INNSBRUCK owes much to a man called Bridges and much to a man called Bach.

The Emperor's new composer

As you wander through the streets of Innsbruck you are sure to notice an ornate house with a glittering roof of copper tiles. This is the *Goldenes Dachl* (the Golden Roof), which was built for the Holy Roman Emperor Maximilian I to celebrate his marriage in 1494. Innsbruck was the heart of the Emperor's domains: when he died in 1519 an elaborate tomb was built for him in the Hofkirche in Innsbruck; however, his body was actually buried somewhere else, so the tomb has to settle for being a cenotaph.

In 1496 Emperor Maximilian employed a new court composer called Heinrich Isaac. Isaac was Flemish by birth but his work as a musician took him to many parts of Europe. He spent much time in Italy, including a spell working for Lorenzo de' Medici; he was in Florence when he died in 1517. Perhaps because he travelled so much, his name is recorded in many different forms: Ysaak, Ysac, Yzac.

Heinrich Isaac
1450–1517

One of Isaac's most enduring compositions was a song called *Innsbruck, ich muss dich lassen* ('Innsbruck I must leave you'). It is not clear whether he actually wrote the tune himself—some scholars declare it is a folk-melody—but he certainly did some arrangements of it for four-part choir, and it is these arrangements that made the song popular. The words are a lament for having to leave the city, which is addressed as if it were a beautiful woman:

> *Innsbruck, I must leave you....*
> *I will be forever yours,*
> *Always faithful...*

Unlike the stern Calvinists of Geneva, the German reformers of the Church who followed in the footsteps of Martin Luther were happy to take secular songs like Isaac's and re-work them for use in a sacred context. Luther himself used many popular melodies, folk-songs, nursery rhymes and so on, adapting them to help congregations praise God with music all could understand. In doing this he was reacting against the complexities of medieval polyphony which had come to dominate the music of the Church, but which the reformers believed obscured the meaning of the words being sung. It seems to have been a German priest called Johannes Hesse who adapted Heinrich Isaac's song for sacred use. Hesse was a contemporary of Luther's who converted to Protestantism in 1523. His version of the Innsbruck song begins '*O Welt, ich muss dich lassen*'—'O World, I must leave you'. Parts of Hesse's text are virtually identical to the original as set by Isaac, with just a few words changed to turn it from a secular love-song into a hymn of other-worldly piety. There is a story that it was written as a comfort for convicted criminals who were awaiting execution and were therefore about to leave the world for real.

Hesse's hymn was published as a pamphlet in 1555 (after both Hesse and Isaac had died), and it appeared in a hymn-book soon after. Over the years the melody has been paired with various texts. J S Bach used the tune as a chorale melody in a number of works, including his *St Matthew Passion*, where he transformed it with his miraculous harmony.

The Yattendon Hymnal

It is one of Bach's arrangements of this chorale that has found its way into English hymn-books, largely thanks to the poet Robert Bridges, who included it in *The Yattendon Hymnal*.

Bridges had moved to Yattendon, in Berkshire, when he was recovering from a bout of pneumonia that almost killed him. He soon became active in the local church, taking a particular interest in the way music was used in worship there and appointing himself precentor—a title usually reserved for the clergyman who is responsible for the music in a cathedral. Working with the artist and composer Harry Ellis Wooldridge, he embarked on producing a hymn-book for use in Yattendon Church. It was initially published as four instalments, beginning in 1895.

Robert Bridges (1844–1930) was born in Kent and educated at Eton—where his friends included the composer Hubert Parry—and Corpus Christi College, Oxford, where he met and befriended Gerald Manley Hopkins. After a period spent travelling he enrolled as a medical student in St Bartholomew's Hospital in London. He failed his medical exams in 1873 but continued his studies later in Dublin, and went on to work as a physician in Bart's, and also in Great Ormond Street and the Royal Northern Hospital, Islington.

He had been writing poetry at least since his Oxford days. A bout of pneumonia in 1881 forced him to take an extended period of sick-leave; during this time he realised that the wealth he had inherited from his family was enough for him to live on without his physician's salary, so from then on he decided to devote his life to writing. In 1882 he moved to Yattendon in Berkshire. He became Poet Laureate in 1913, after Rudyard Kipling had been offered the post and refused it.

Like Percy Dearmer and Ralph Vaughan Williams a decade later, Bridges was motivated (at least in part) by his dislike of that old warhorse of Victorian hymn-books, *Hymns Ancient & Modern*. To begin with his aim seems to have been purely musical. He declared that he wanted 'to provide better settings of the hymns than those in use', selecting only tunes that would fit the words of hymns found in *A&M*. Later, as the hymnal grew, he began to pick tunes on their own merit. Where there were no existing lyrics to fit these tunes, he would write his own: either completely original texts, or translations of hymns from Latin and other languages. In this way he preserved tunes that had previously been associated with second-rate verse:

> In some cases [...] the musician, out of despair or even contempt for the doggrel [sic] offered to him, has composed a fine tune quite independent of the words to which it was dedicated, and such tunes have been silent ever since they were composed.

The Yattendon Hymnal was a remarkable book. Unlike Dearmer's *The English Hymnal*, the intention was never to produce a comprehensive collection: there are just 100 hymns (compared to more than 600 in *The English Hymnal*). The Yattendon book was beautifully produced: designed by Wooldridge and printed on hand-made paper using an old typeface. The music engraving is extraordinary, using a style that is obviously meant to look handwritten, though it is clear and easy to read. The stave-lines of the ancient plainchant melodies are printed in red. It is a book that was intended to be a work of art itself, not merely a tool.

Heinrich Isaac's tune appears twice in *The Yattendon Hymnal*: once in its original form (no. 82) and once in Bach's chorale harmonisation (no. 83; see illustration on page 37). The older setting is given the words 'My heart is filled with longing', which Bridges wrote himself 'after François Amiel'. In the body of the *Hymnal* the tunes are not given names; but in the notes at the back of the book Bridges remarks that 'As a hymn-tune the melody is known as INSBRUCK [*sic*], from the initial word of the original secular song'

Bach's version of the tune (which Bridges—astonishingly—claims 'must rank in an inferior order of beauty to Isaac's song') is also set to a free translation by Bridges: this time, of a lyric by Paul Gerhardt (1607–1676) which begins '*Nun ruhen alle Wälder*'. There is a more faithful translation of this poem by Catherine Winkworth that begins 'Now all the woods are sleeping'; Bridges' hymn is more an impression than an actual translation. His dense, distilled phrases are difficult yet memorable, with such vivid images as 'Shade creeps o'er wild and wood' and the wonderfully strange 'This life he disesteemeth'. From *The Yattendon Hymnal* it passed into *The English Hymnal*, and eventually found its way into a later edition (1950) of *Hymns Ancient & Modern*, the very book that Bridges was reacting against when he published his own collection.

Innsbruck, I must leave you

Before we leave Innsbruck, let us climb the countless steps up to the top of the *Stadtturm* or City Tower. From here, if you have a head for heights, you can look down on the city with its snow-covered roofs and medieval streets. Just outside the city, seemingly almost close enough to touch, are the Alpine peaks, white and indomitable, through which the Inn Valley winds. It is almost a shock to see the massive mountains rising up so near to the edges of human habitation.

Innsbruck's Christmas-card streets with their fairytale figures and their warm, welcoming shops and cafés are a comforting haven amid those great rocky peaks. No wonder Heinrich Isaac or Yzak was so sorry to leave this city. Yet if he had not left Innsbruck, Bach and Bridges would never have given us INNSBRUCK.

❖

INNSBRUCK

MANY OF THE TUNES in this book, like INNSBRUCK, were not originally meant to be used for worship. On the next stage of our journey we will learn the story of one of the most popular of all tunes, one in which neither the words nor the music were supposed to be sung as a hymn.

INNSBRUCK, from *The Yattendon Hymnal;* **harmony by J S Bach**

Chapter 4

REPTON

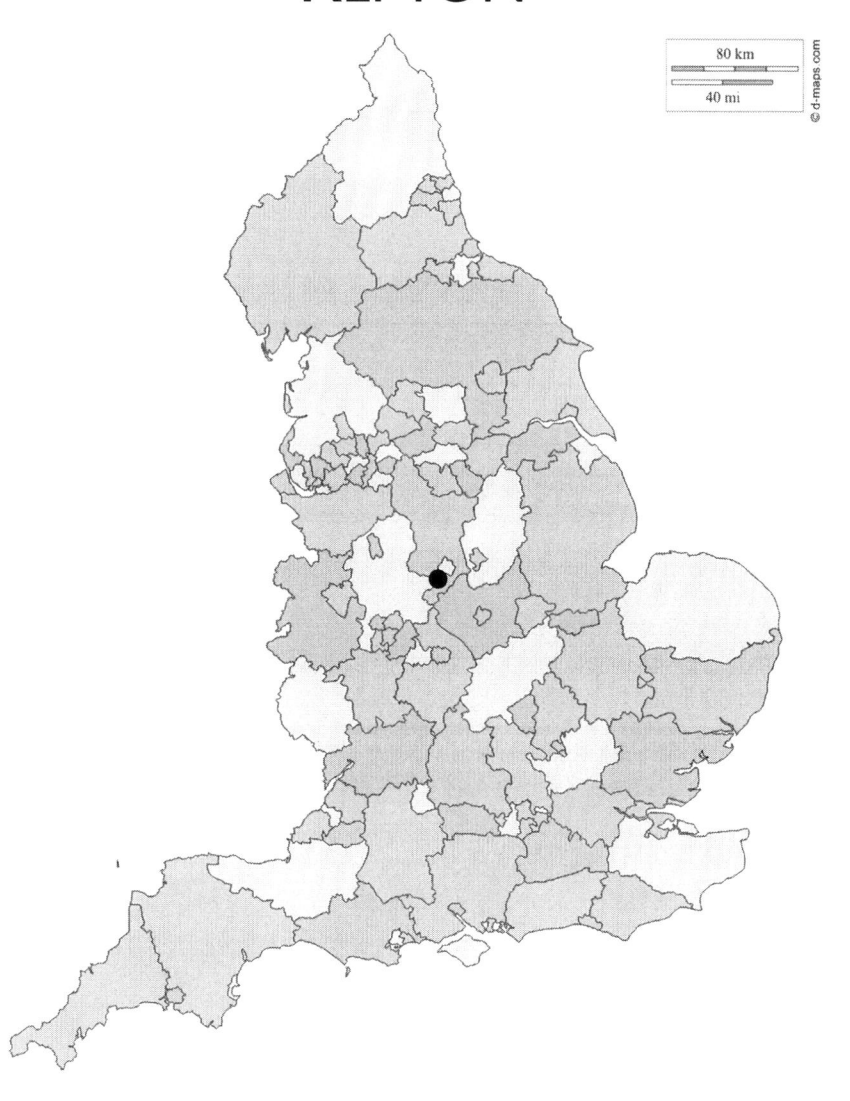

REPTON

Dear Lord and father of mankind

Dear Lord and Fath-er of man-kind, for-give our fool-ish ways;

CHARLES HUBERT HASTINGS PARRY 1848-1918

IN ANGLO-SAXON TIMES England was divided into seven kingdoms: Northumbria, Mercia, East Anglia, Essex, Kent, Sussex, and Wessex. Repton, a village in Derbyshire, proclaims itself the 'historic capital of Mercia', a region which roughly corresponded to what we now call the Midlands—though at certain points in history it stretched down as far as Bristol in the west and London in the east.

In 653 the Mercian royal family were converted to Christianity in Repton by some priests from Northumbria; subsequently they built an abbey at Repton, which thrived until it was destroyed by Vikings in 873. The crypt of St Wystan's Church survives, and is widely held to be one of the architectural wonders of the Anglo-Saxon world.

Repton Priory

The abbey was replaced by a priory in the 12th century; this lasted until the Dissolution of the Monasteries by Henry VIII in 1538. The site of Repton Priory passed to Thomas Thacker, the steward of Thomas Cromwell, and then to Thacker's son, Gilbert. When Queen Mary came to the throne in 1553 Gilbert Thacker was worried that the Priory might go back to its original, Catholic, function, so he had it knocked down. As Thacker put it, 'He would destroy the nest, for fear the birds should build therein again.'

The land on which the Priory had stood, and the few remaining buildings that were still standing, were sold in 1557 to the executors of

Sir John Port of Etwall. Port (c.1510–1557) was a lawyer and statesman whose father (also Sir John) had been an eminent judge and an associate of Richard Sutton, the founder of Brasenose College, Oxford. The younger Sir John was employed by Thomas Cromwell for a time, and was twice Member of Parliament for Derbyshire. He had five children—two sons and three daughters—but his sons did not survive beyond infancy, so when he himself died in 1557 his estate was broken up. In his will he left funds for Brasenose College, and he also bequeathed money to found alms-houses in Etwall and a school in nearby Repton, whose scholars were to pray daily for his soul.

Repton school

The school was set up in 1559 on the site of the old Priory, for which Port's executors paid £37 10s. It is still flourishing to this day as an independent school; and no doubt the students still pray for the repose of Sir John Port every day. Former pupils of the school include the athlete Harold Abrahams, the actor Basil Rathbone, Michael Ramsey (the 100th Archbishop of Canterbury), Graeme Garden and Jeremy Clarkson. Headmasters of the school have included two other Archbishops of Canterbury: William Temple and his successor Geoffrey Fisher.

The Headmaster of Repton from 1854 to 1874 was Steuart Adolphus Pears. He did much to revive and expand the school, and is known as its 'second founder' (the first being Sir John Port). Among the things he did was to have a new chapel built. This was opened in 1859; and in the same year the first edition of the *Repton School Hymn-book* was brought out for use in the chapel. This book contained 103 hymns. Subsequent editions enlarged the collection until it included 265 hymns. From 1906 the school adopted *Hymns Ancient & Modern* as its standard hymn-book, but it continued to produce a supplement which contained hymns not found in the main book.

The Repton hymn-book

By 1924, when Geoffrey Fisher was headmaster, this supplement had become a slender book of 69 hymns. These were numbered from 800 to 868 (presumably to avoid confusion with hymn numbers in *Ancient & Modern*). Among these are many hymns that have since become familiar, including an early appearance of JERUSALEM.

Several of the tunes in the *Repton School Hymn-book* were composed by the music master, Dr George Gilbert Stocks; and in many cases he named these tunes after places, such as CHARING CROSS, BRETBY and ETWALL (the last two being villages near Repton). Most of Stocks' own tunes were intended to be sung in unison, to make them suitable for hearty singing by a chapelful of boys.

Stocks also adapted existing tunes to fit the words of hymn-tunes. Part of his motivation in doing this seems to have been to introduce the boys to great works of classical music. There is one tune called VERDI which is an arrangement of the *Lachrymosa* from Verdi's *Requiem*, set to words by H A Martin:

> *O Rock of Ages, one Foundation*
>   *On which the living Church doth rest—*
> *The Church, whose walls are strong salvation,*
>   *Whose gates are praise—Thy name be blest.*

Stocks gave the name REPTON SCHOOL to a tune by the Revd J Pears. But he kept the one-word name REPTON for a tune by his old tutor from Oxford, Sir Charles Hubert Hastings Parry.

Sir Hubert Parry

Parry was born in Bournemouth in 1848 and grew up at the family home, Highnam in Gloucestershire, less than forty miles from Down Ampney and less than fifteen from Cranham. He went to Eton in 1861 and to Exeter College, Oxford, in 1867, where he studied law and modern history. On graduating from Oxford in 1870, wishing to please his father and his prospective in-laws, he went to work at Lloyd's of London as an underwriter; he remained in the world of insurance for a further seven years.

Meanwhile he was pursuing his real passion: music. He had met S S Wesley at Winchester Cathedral before he went to Eton, and had begun piano and harmony lessons with Edward Brind, the organist at Highnam church. While at school he founded the Eton College Musical Society and found time, when not playing the Eton Wall Game (at which he excelled), to pass the Oxford BMus degree.

Sir Charles Hubert Hastings Parry 1848–1918

While he was still at Lloyd's, Parry was noticed by George Grove, a civil engineer and writer on music, who was working on a monumental reference work that would become *Grove's Dictionary of Music and Musicians*. In 1875 Grove appointed Parry as Assistant Editor of the Dictionary: he was eventually to submit 123 articles for the book. In 1882 Grove was appointed Director of the new Royal College of Music, and in the following year he took on Parry as Professor of Composition and Musical History. When Grove retired in 1895 Parry succeeded him as Director. Among his pupils were Henry Walford Davies, Ralph Vaughan Williams, Gustav Holst, Frank Bridge and John Ireland; his articles in *Grove* were also a huge influence on the self-taught Elgar.

Parry had been a keen sportsman when at school. The *Dictionary of National Biography* tells us nonchalantly that he was in the Oppidan wall eleven; and with a little digging I have discovered that an Oppidan Scholar is a boy who has attained notable achievement in examinations, though perhaps not as outstanding as the King's Scholars. On St Andrew's Day each year the Oppidans and the Kings Scholars have an annual match of the Wall Game. This is a sort of cross between rugby,

Quidditch and a firing-squad which involves not only a wall but also a garden door and a tree, and uses such arcane vocabulary as 'calx' and 'furk'.

In later life Parry continued to enjoy sport. He had successes racing his 88-foot ketch *Wanderer*, and is the only eminent composer to have been elected a member of the Royal Yacht Squadron, to which he was admitted in 1907; the Squadron possesses copies of *Grove* and Parry's own *The Music of the Seventeenth Century* which he presented to them

The story of Judith

The tune that Stocks named REPTON was taken from an oratorio by Parry, called *Judith, or the Regeneration of Manasseh*.

Manasseh was a king of Judah who, according to the Second Book of Kings in the Bible, 'did that which was evil in the sight of the LORD, after the abominations of the heathen, whom the LORD cast out before the children of Israel.' Judith was an Israelite woman who has a whole book to herself in the Apocrypha, the collection of books that are not quite in the Bible but still somehow within its orbit. In the Book of Judith, she was a widow, whose husband Manasses had died some years earlier when supervising workers in the field on a very hot day. The Assyrian army, led by General Holofernes, was poised to attack the Children of Israel; but Judith went into the enemy camp and used her beauty to get into Holofernes' tent. The Assyrian general, beguiled by her good looks, had a great feast prepared in her honour, and 'drank more wine than he had drunk at any time in one day since he was born.' After the feast, with Holofernes slumped on his bed in a drunken mess and all the servants gone, Judith took a sword and 'smote twice upon his neck with all her might, and she took away his head from him.' She slipped the head into her bag and made her escape.

The Assyrians, when they found out that Holofernes was dead, were thrown into confusion; and the Israelites lived happily ever after—at least until the next lot of aggressive neighbours moved in.

There is no suggestion that Judith's late husband Manasses was the same person as King Manasseh. However, Humphrey Prideaux, who was Dean of Norwich in the early eighteenth century, asserted in his book *The Old and New Testament connected* that the events described in the Book of Judith happened during the reign of Manasseh. Parry picked up on this idea for his oratorio. Originally he did not intend Judith to be the central character, because, as he put it, 'though her heroism is most admirable, the sanguinary catastrophe of the story is neither artistically attractive nor suitable for introduction into a work in the Oratorio form.' But Judith was too interesting to be kept on the sidelines, and he soon found himself putting her centre stage.

A good old-fashioned oratorio

Parry was not the first composer to use Judith as a subject for an oratorio: there is also a *Judith* by Thomas Arne (the composer of *Rule, Britannia*). A song from Arne's work was performed at a concert in 1767 accompanied by a pianoforte: the first recorded public use of a piano in England.

Parry's *Judith* was completed in 1888. It was commissioned for a festival in Birmingham after the immense success of *Blest Pair of Sirens*, a setting of Milton's poem *At a Solemn Musick*, which was written for Queen Victoria's Golden Jubilee in 1887. Always inclined to question conventional religious ideas, Parry considered a number of secular themes for his new work: he even thought of writing something on the subject of Christopher Columbus. But the public—and the Birmingham festival committee in particular—wanted a good old-fashioned Old Testament oratorio like Handel's *Solomon* or Mendelssohn's *Elijah*. So Parry obliged with *Judith*.

However reluctantly the composer had embarked on it, the oratorio was a great success; though George Bernard Shaw, for one, felt that the popular demand for Biblical choral works was distracting Parry from writing symphonies and the like, which Shaw thought would use his talents better.

Posterity seems to have agreed with Shaw. As far as I can see there is no complete recording of *Judith*, and live performances seem to be non-existent too. Perhaps it wasn't Parry's finest work after all.

The Queen's ballad

There is one passage, however, that has often been recorded. It is an aria (or 'ballad' as Parry calls it) sung by King Manasseh's wife, the splendidly-named Queen Meshullemeth. While the worshippers of Moloch are working themselves into a frenzy and demanding the royal children as human sacrifices for their bloodthirsty god, the queen is shut in the palace with the children. To comfort them she tells them the story of how long ago Moses led the children of Israel out of Egypt, through the Red Sea and across the desert to the Promised Land, aided by God. The words of the song are (as far as I have been able to discover) by Parry himself:

> *Long since in Egypt's plenteous land*
> *Our fathers were oppressed;*
> *But God, whose chosen folk they were,*
> *Smote those who long enslaved them there,*
> *And all their woes redressed.*
>
> *The Red Sea stayed them not at all,*
> *Nor depths of liquid green;*
> *On either hand a mighty wall*
> *Of waters clear rose at his call,*
> *And they passed through between.*
>
> *In deserts wild they wandered long,*
> *They sinned and went astray;*
> *But yet his arm to help was strong,*

O Little Town

He pardoned them tho' they did wrong,
And brought them on their way.

At last to this good land they came,
With fruitful plenty blest;
Here glorious men won endless fame,
Here God made holy Zion's name,
And here he gave them rest.

To which the children reply:

Oh, may we ne'er forget what he hath done,
Nor prove unmindful of his love,
That, like the constant sun,
On Israel hath shone,
And sent down blessings from above.

The main part of the ballad, sung by the Queen, is set to a beautiful and memorable melody in which the last line of each stanza is repeated. It is because of this tune that this is the one section from *Judith* that has been often recorded: not only for its intrinsic beauty, but because the melody is much better known in a different context. For this is the tune that Dr Stocks included in his school's hymn supplement under the name of REPTON.

Soma

In Dr Stocks' book the tune is used for the hymn we know as *Dear Lord and Father of mankind*. Like *Jerusalem*, these words were never meant to be a hymn: indeed, it is likely that their author may well have been saddened to find they were being used in this way.

The author in question was John Greenleaf Whittier. Whittier was an American Quaker born in 1807 who was a keen opponent of slavery and a founder member of the American Anti-Slavery Society. A number of his poems have been used as hymns, though he himself said 'I am not really a hymn-writer, for the very good reason that I know nothing of music. Only a few of my pieces were written for singing.'

In 1872 he published a poem called *The Brewing of Soma*. Soma is a mythical drink referred to in the Vedas, the ancient Hindu scriptures. According to Hymn XLVIII of the Rig-Veda, as translated by Ralph T H Griffith (1896):

We have drunk Soma and become immortal;
we have attained the light, the Gods discovered.
Now what may foeman's malice do to harm us?
What, O Immortal, mortal man's deception?

The word *soma* is Sanskrit, and it is distantly—very distantly—related to a whole royal-straight-flush of English words: *sap, sip, sop* and *sup*. Its basic meaning is 'juice': in the Vedic tradition soma is made from the juice of a plant.

In his novel *Brave New World*, Aldous Huxley describes a dystopian society in which selective breeding has produced distinct classes of citizen. All these citizens are encouraged to take a drug called Soma, a non-addictive, harmless narcotic which, as Huxley puts it, has 'all the advantages of Christianity and alcohol; none of their defects.' Huxley himself experimented with real drugs, as described in his book *The Doors of Perception*, a title taken from William Blake's *The Marriage of Heaven and Hell*. (Jim Morrison's band The Doors, incidentally, took its name from Huxley's book.) The Soma of *Brave New World* is clearly a reference to the mythical life-giving drink of the Vedas.

John Greenleaf Whittier
1807–1892

Sensual transports

John Greenleaf Whittier's reference to Soma was every bit as satirical and polemic as Aldous Huxley's. As a Quaker, Whittier was concerned with listening for the voice of God. At meetings of the Society of Friends there is more silence than talking: there is no music; there are no hymns. Whittier clearly did not disapprove entirely of music: he said that only *a few* of his poems were written for singing, but there were at least those few. What worried him was that all the noise that music created could drive away that silence which is needed to hear God speaking. In this sense, he saw music in worship as part of the same tradition as ancient pagan rituals which involved wild dancing, or the taking of mind-expanding drugs. This is the context of *The Brewing of Soma*.

Here is the poem in full:

The fagots blazed, the cauldron's smoke
Up through the green wood curled;
'Bring honey from the hollow oak,
Brink milky sap,' the brewers spoke,
In the childhood of the world.
And brewed they well or brewed they ill,
The priests thrust in their rods,
First tasted, and then drank their fill,
And shouted, with one voice and will,
'Behold, the drink of the gods!'

They drank, and lo! in heart and brain
A new, glad life began;
The gray of hair grew young again,
The sick man laughed away his pain,
The cripple leaped and ran.

'Drink, mortals, what the gods have sent,

Forget you long annoy.'
So sang the priests, From tent to tent
The Soma's sacred madness went,
A storm of drunken joy.

Then knew each rapt inebriate
A winged and glorious birth,
Soared upward, with strange joy elate,
Beat, with dazed head, Varuna's gate,
And sobered, sank to earth.

The land with Soma's praises rang;
On Gihon's banks of shade
Its hymns the dusky maidens sang;
In joy of life or mortal pang
All men to Soma prayed.

The morning twilight of the race
Sends down these matin psalms;
And still with wondering eyes we trace
The simple prayers to Soma's grace,
That vedic verse embalms.

As in the child-world's early year,
Each after age has striven
By music, incense, vigils drear,
And trance, to bring the skies more near,
Or lift men up to heaven!

Some fever of the blood and brain,
Some self-exalting spell,
The scourger's keen delight of pain,

O Little Town

the Dervish dance, the Orphic strain,
The wild-haired Bacchant's yell, -

The desert's hair-grown hermit sunk
The saner brute below;
The naked Santon, haschish-drunk,
The cloister madness of the monk,
The fakir's torture show!

And yet the past comes round again,
And new doth old fulfil;
In sensual transports wild as vain
We brew in many a Christian fane
The heathen Soma still!

Dear Lord and Father of mankind,
Forgive our foolish ways!
Reclothe us in our rightful mind,
In purer lives Thy service find,
In deeper reverence, praise.

In simple trust like theirs who heard
Beside the Syrian sea
The gracious calling of the Lord,
Let us, like them, without a word
Rise up and follow Thee.

O Sabbath rest by Galilee!
O calm of hills above,
Where Jesus knelt to share with Thee
The silence of eternity
Interpreted by love!

With that deep hush subduing all
Our words and works that drown
The tender whisper of Thy call,
And noiseless let Thy blessing fall
As fell Thy manna down.

Drop thy still dews of quietness,
Till all our strivings cease;
Take from our souls the strain and stress,
And let our ordered lives confess
The beauty of Thy peace.

Breathe through the heats of our desire
Thy coolness and Thy balm;
Let sense be dumb, let flesh retire;
Speak through the earthquake, wind, and fire,
O still, small voice of calm!

So the words that are familiar to us as *Dear Lord and father of mankind* are just the last few stanzas of this much longer poem. In the context of the rest of the poem the old familiar phrases like 'silence of eternity', 'beauty of thy peace' and 'still small voice of calm' can be seen as a call for not just peace but silence: an escape from drugs, and dance, and even singing. Along with the 'storm of drunken joy' Whittier places 'music, incense, vigils drear', the 'Orphic strain' and hymns, whether sung by dusky maidens or anyone else. It is all part of the 'heathen Soma' that he condemns.

It is odd, then, that his verses have become one of the most popular hymns of all.

These matin psalms

Dear Lord and Father of mankind was first used as a hymn by William Garett Horder, in a book called *Congregational Hymns*, in 1884. It has been sung to a number of tunes, including one called HAMMERSMITH by William Henry Gladstone (1840-1891), son of the great Liberal Prime Minister William Ewart Gladstone. But—in England at least—it is most usually associated with the tune that Dr George Gilbert Stocks adapted from Parry's oratorio Judith, and named REPTON after the school where he was Head of Music.

In 2005 the BBC programme *Songs of Praise* ran a poll to find the nation's favourite hymn. *Dear Lord and Father of mankind* came in second place, after *How great thou art*. I am sure that its popularity is partly due to the beauty and aptness of Parry's tune, as well as Whittier's words.

❖

REPTON is not Parry's only contribution to the repertoire of hymn-tunes. Our next destination is nominally further from home than anywhere else on our journey; but in reality it is in the heart of England. Its story, like that of REPTON, concerns a hymn that was never meant to be a hymn.

Chapter 5
JERUSALEM

JERUSALEM

And did those feet in ancient time

And did those feet in an-cient time walk up-on Eng-land's moun-tains green?

CHARLES HUBERT HASTINGS PARRY 1848-1918

THE CITY OF JERUSALEM is not, of course, a particularly little town. It is not huge compared to the world's mega-cities—its population is somewhat smaller than that of Liverpool—but it does have an incredibly long history, having been settled around six thousand years ago.

The Jerusalem I am concerned with, though, is not really the middle-eastern city, but a metaphorical Jerusalem, symbolic of the City of God: something to aspire to. It is the Jerusalem of the Women's Institute and the Last Night of the Proms, the Jerusalem of sports matches and Armistice Day.

A very peculiar poem

The words of the song we know as *Jerusalem* were never meant to be sung by prommers, or indeed members of the Women's Institute. They are taken from the Preface to a narrative poem by William Blake called *Milton*. In this very strange poem the spirit of John Milton, author of *Paradise Lost*, comes down from Heaven—or whatever ethereal abode he is in—and lands in Lambeth, where he is trodden on by Blake and takes up residence in his foot. It is an odd, mystical poem peopled by characters with names like Los and Ololon. Here is an excerpt to give you a flavour:

> *From Golgonooza the spiritual Four-fold London eternal,*
> *In immense labours & sorrows, ever building, ever falling,*

Thro' Albion's four Forests which overspread all the Earth
From London Stone to Blackheath east: to Hounslow west:
To Finchley north: to Norwood south: and the weights
Of Enitharmon's Loom play lulling cadences on the winds of Albion
From Caithness in the north, to Lizard-point & Dover in the south.
Loud sounds the hammer of Los, & loud his Bellows is heard
Before London to Hampstead's breadths & Highgate's heights, To
Stratford & old Bow, & across to the Gardens of Kensington
On Tyburn's Brook: loud groans Thames beneath the iron Forge
Of Rintrah & Palamabron, of Theotorm & Bromion, to forge the instruments
Of Harvest: The Plow & Harrow to pass over the Nations.

Well. I don't know about you, but I find it hard to take seriously a work that combines the booming high-minded language and rhythms of epic verse with references to Hounslow and Finchley, let alone one that introduces made-up names like Golgonooza.

In the Preface to *Milton* Blake rails against what he calls 'the stolen and perverted writings of Homer & Ovid, of Plato & Cicero'. He calls on the 'young men of the New Age' to rebel against the hypocritical Establishment, whom he refers to as 'hirelings in the Camp, the Court, & the University'. He then ends the Preface with the well-known lines: 'And did those feet in ancient time...'

William Blake
1757–1827

The lyric is not given a title by Blake: it is simply the last part of his Preface, given in verse. It refers to a legend that claims Joseph of Arimathea once brought Jesus to England and visited Glastonbury. In the Gospels, Joseph was the man who made his own tomb available for Jesus's body after the Crucifixion; according to the legend, he was a tin merchant and came to England for trade, bringing the young Jesus with him. His name also crops up in the stories surrounding the Holy Grail.

The famous 'dark Satanic Mills' in Blake's poem have been interpreted in many different ways. Some read this phrase as a reference to the Industrial Revolution, with its mechanised cotton mills and flour mills bringing wealth to a few and poverty to the many. Another point of view says that the Satanic Mills are the 'Camp, the Court and the University' to which Blake refers in his Preface to *Milton*, and in particular the Universities of Oxford and Cambridge, which set such store by the 'stolen and perverted' Classics. Blake's formal schooling ended at the age of ten, and he seems to have believed that he was better off (spiritually) as a result. Personally, I wonder if the phrase 'satanic mills' came to his mind through association with the name Milton: Satan is, of course, a major character in *Paradise Lost*.

The music of *Jerusalem*

It is unlikely that Blake would have intended his lyric to be sung. It is unthinkable that he would have approved of the status it now has as a statement of national pride in the same vein as *God Save the Queen*, *Rule, Britannia* and *Land of Hope and Glory*; or even that it would regularly feature in hymn-books of the Established Church of England.

A choral setting of these words, with the title *England's Pleasant Land*, was composed by Sir Henry Walford Davies in 1907. Walford Davies was later to succeed Sir Edward Elgar as Master of the King's Musick, and he is known to choirs as the composer of *God be in my head* and an alternative tune for *O little town of Bethlehem*.

But the tune that will forever be associated with Blake's poem from the Preface to *Milton* is by Sir Charles Hubert Hastings Parry.

It seems to have been Robert Bridges who suggested to Parry that he should set *Jerusalem* to music. In 1915 Bridges, who had been made Poet Laureate in 1913, brought out a collection of poems and philosophical essays by various authors, in English and French, called *The Spirit of Man*. This was published with the intention of raising the morale of the nation with uplifting thoughts. In his preface to this collection, Bridges explains his motive as the cause of liberty in the face of the terrible catastrophe of the Great War that was raging:

> Britons have ever fought well for their country, and their country's Cause is the high Cause of Freedom and Honour. That fairest earthly fame, the fame of Freedom, is inseparable from the names of Albion, Britain, England: it has gone out to America and the Antipodes, hallowing the names of Canada, Australia, and New Zealand; it has found a new home in Africa: and this heritage is our glory and happiness. We can therefore be happy in our sorrows, happy even in the death of our beloved who fall in the fight; for they die nobly, as heroes and saints die, with hearts and hands unstained by hatred or wrong.

Bridges was almost seventy at the outbreak of war in July 1914, so he did not witness first-hand the horrors that were depicted by younger poets like Sassoon and Owen.

The verse we know as *Jerusalem* is Number 411 in *The Spirit of Man*, sandwiched between a passage from Milton's *Areopagitica* (a speech against censorship) and lines from Sir Walter Scott's *The Lay of the Last Minstrel*:

> *Breathes there the man, with soul so dead,*
> *Who never to himself hath said,*
> *'This is my own, my native land!'*

Bridges asked Parry to set Blake's words to music for a meeting of Fight for Right, a movement dedicated to encouraging Britain's involvement in the Great War. Parry duly did so, and was evidently pleased with the result, but became a little uneasy with the jingoistic aims and tone of Fight for Right and nearly withdrew his score, only relenting so as not to disappoint Bridges and Walford Davies, who was to conduct the first performance.

Over the next two years the song was taken up by the women's suffrage movement, and Parry gave his approval for it to be used as the Women Voters' hymn; indeed, he assigned the copyright in the song to the National Union of Women's Suffrage Societies. Later the copyright was passed to the Women's Institute, with which it is still very closely associated.

From anthem to hymn

Jerusalem quickly became a popular song. Parry arranged it for orchestra in 1918, and a few years later, in 1922, Elgar did his own orchestral arrangement: it is Elgar's that is usually played at the Proms.

It was around this time that it started to find its way into hymn books. In 1925 it appeared in *Songs of Praise*, a book edited by Percy Dearmer and Ralph Vaughan Williams and intended primarily for use in schools. This seems to have been the first time it was included in a nationally available hymn-book, though its use as a hymn was already established. For example, in 1924 it appeared in the *Repton School Hymn-book*, alongside the first use of the tune REPTON.

❖

A LONG WAY FROM JERUSALEM, in an authentically green and pleasant part of England, we find a 'little town' that inspired another patriotic tune: one which has links to a place so far away it is literally out of this world.

Chapter 6

THAXTED

THAXTED

I vow to thee, my country

I vow to thee, my count-ry, all earth-ly things a-bove,

GUSTAV HOLST 1874-1934

THAXTED IS A TOWN in rural Essex, about five or six miles southeast of Saffron Walden, in a neighbourhood sprinkled with splendid place-names such as Ugley, Maggots End, Pleasant Valley, Wimbish and Wendens Ambo. The name Thaxted seems to mean *thatch-place*. The landscape here is not exactly hilly, but neither is it as dead flat as some other parts of East Anglia. If you are coming from the south, as I did one bright autumn morning, you will look in vain for some sign that you are getting close to the town, until suddenly you come over the brow of a modest hill and see the brickwork and white sails of John Webb's windmill, and next to it the imposing spire of Thaxted's church. This church, dedicated to St John the Baptist, St Mary and St Laurence, has been called the finest parish church in the country, and some have dubbed it the 'cathedral of Essex'.

Thaxted can trace its history back more than a thousand years. I suppose some of the old buildings in the town centre might have had straight lines and right angles once, but today they are all just a little bit wonky and seem to lean against each other for support. Many of the houses are painted in bold, cheerful colours.

Our Mr Von

Gustav von Holst—he still had a 'von' in those days—first visited Thaxted while on a walking tour in 1913, and fell in love with the place.

O Little Town

The following year he and his wife Isobel moved to Monk Street, about a mile to the south of Thaxted. It was a place of beauty and tranquillity that captivated Holst:

> It stood high above the surrounding cornfields and meadows and willow trees, with a view of the church spire in the distance. It was so quiet that we could hear the bees in the dark red clover beyond the garden hedge. We could watch the meadow grass being scythed, and in the cornfields we saw the farmer sowing the seed by hand, scattering it in the breeze as he strode up and down. The only traffic along what is now the main road was the carrier's cart which stopped every few hundred yards to pick up parcels and passengers on Wednesday afternoons: on the other days, people walked.

It was here in Monk Street that he wrote his most famous work, *The Planets*. This began as *Seven Pieces for Large Orchestra*, and was originally a response to the landscape around Thaxted: the association with the planets was added later.

Gustav Holst (1874–1934) was born in Cheltenham. He studied music at the Royal College of Music, where his teachers included Parry and Stanford. It was here he met Ralph Vaughan Williams, a fellow-student at the RCM; they formed a close and lifelong friendship.

To supplement the meagre income he earned from his compositions, Holst took teaching posts, most famously at St Paul's Girls' School in Hammersmith and also as Director of Music at Morley College (a post that was later held by Sir Michael Tippett).

As well as *The Planets*, Holst composed songs, operas, ballet music, choral works, chamber music, and of course hymn-tunes, of which the best known are CRANHAM (for *In the bleak midwinter*) and THAXTED.

When the Great War broke out, Holst was declared unfit for military service, so could not join up. During the war he dropped the 'von' from his surname, presumably because it looked too German; though in fact he was of Scandinavian and Russian ancestry, and he himself was as English as they come, having been born in Cheltenham. The 'von' had, in any case, been added to the family name by Holst's father, Adolph, at a time when German music was fashionable, and appearing *more* German was possibly an advantage for a piano teacher in Cheltenham. The church choir at Thaxted affectionately referred to Holst as 'our Mr Von'; but some of the neighbours were suspicious and reported him to the police, who fortunately concluded he did not represent a threat.

'The Manse', Holst's house in Thaxted

In 1917 the Holsts moved into Thaxted proper, to a house called 'The Steps', which was later renamed 'The Manse'. It is painted pale blue and is adorned with a plaque commemorating Holst's time there. Gustav had already become friendly with the vicar of Thaxted, Conrad Le Dispenser Noel, who was famous—some would say notorious—for his Socialist views. He even hung the Red Flag in his church, next to the flag of St George, till he was ordered to take it down by the Church authorities. In 1916 Holst and Noel had established a Whitsuntide music festival which continued till 1918; its heir in present-day Thaxted is a thriving festival which began in 1980. Conrad Noel was also responsible for founding the Thaxted Morris Men in 1914 as part of the folk-dance revival led by Cecil Sharp. They are still dancing to this day, and proclaim themselves 'the oldest revival side in the country'.

> **Cecil Sharp (1859–1924)** was at the forefront of a movement whose aim was to revive and preserve our national folk heritage, both song and dance. In the early years of the twentieth century, mechanical means of recording music were in their infancy, and the only practical way for Sharp and his collaborators to capture folk music was to go out into the villages, listen carefully to the songs and write the tunes down. They referred to this process as 'collecting' folk-songs, much as Victorian gentlemen such as Charles Darwin, fifty years earlier, would go out and collect beetles.
>
> Sharp was a leading light of the Folk-Song Society, founded in 1898, whose Vice-Presidents included Hubert Parry and Charles Villiers Stanford.

City of God

In 1918 Holst's friend Ralph Vaughan Williams sent him a poem by Sir Cecil Spring-Rice. Lucy Broadwood had seen the poem and sent it to

Vaughan Williams, suggesting he might like to set it to music. Vaughan Williams was too busy at the time, so forwarded the poem to Holst. (Some years later Vaughan Williams did get round to writing a tune for the poem, which he called ABINGER after a place not far from his home in Leith Hill. It was included in *Songs of Praise* (1931) but has never had anything like the success of Holst's tune.)

The poem had begun life in 1912 under the title *Urbs Dei* (City of God). Spring-Rice, a diplomat, had written it while British Ambassador to Sweden. In its original form it begins:

> *I heard my country calling, away across the sea,*
> *Across the waste of waters she calls and calls to me;*
> *Her sword is girded at her side, her helmet on her head;*
> *And round her feet are lying the dying and the dead;*
> *I hear the noise of battle, the thunder of her guns,*
> *I haste to thee my mother, a son among her sons.*

It is a patriotic poem, specifically about his homeland, with the references to 'her sword' and 'her helmet' recalling the traditional image of Britannia as a woman dressed for war. Yet it is not a warlike poem, but rather one filled with compassion for those who suffer in war: 'the dying and the dead'.

In 1913 Spring-Rice was posted to Washington as the British Ambassador to the United States. The US Secretary of State at that time, with whom Spring-Rice naturally had many dealings in the course of his work, was William Jennings Bryan. Bryan was an unswerving opponent of Darwinism, believing that the idea of 'survival of the fittest' was partly responsible for the aggressive militarisation of Germany. He was later to be involved in the famous 'Scopes Monkey Trial' of 1925 in which a teacher was prosecuted

Cecil Spring-Rice 1859–1918

for teaching the theory of evolution in a state-funded school; Bryan spoke for the prosecution at this trial.

Bryan was a pacifist, whose proudest achievement was the 'thirty peace treaties' which, as he put it, 'make war practically impossible between this country and these thirty governments, representing nearly three-fourths of all the people of the world.' Among the one-quarter of the world's population *not* covered by these treaties was, unfortunately, Germany. Bryan had resigned as Secretary of State in 1915 when President Woodrow Wilson had made worryingly warlike comments towards Germany after the sinking of the *Lusitania*. When the USA entered the war in 1917, however, Bryan graciously offered to join the military in whatever capacity the President wished: an offer that was declined.

The Two Fatherlands

In 1917 Cecil Spring-Rice left his Washington post, and on his departure Bryan presented him with a book called *Heart to Heart Appeals*, a collection of his political speeches and writings reflecting, among other things, his belief that conciliation between countries was always better than aggression.

Something about Bryan's text inspired Spring-Rice to revise his poem *Urbs Dei*, discarding the first verse quoted above and adding a new one. The full poem in its revised form is as follows:

> *I vow to thee, my country, all earthly things above,*
> *Entire and whole and perfect, the service of my love;*
> *The love that asks no question, the love that stands the test,*
> *That lays upon the altar the dearest and the best;*
> *The love that never falters, the love that pays the price,*
> *The love that makes undaunted the final sacrifice.*
>
> *And there's another country, I've heard of long ago,*
> *Most dear to them that love her, most great to them that know;*

We may not count her armies, we may not see her King;
Her fortress is a faithful heart, her pride is suffering;
And soul by soul and silently her shining bounds increase,
And her ways are ways of gentleness, and all her paths are peace.

This is the version, with the title *The Two Fatherlands*, that Lucy Broadwood had seen in 1918. Just like Vaughan Williams, Holst was too busy to compose any new music for it, but he realised that he already had a tune which would fit it rather well: the grand melody in *Jupiter, the Bringer of Jollity* from *The Planets*.

Thaxted church, 'The cathedral of Essex'

In 1921 Holst published *The Two Fatherlands* as a unison song with orchestral accompaniment, using the tune from *Jupiter*. It first appeared as a hymn in *Songs of Praise* in 1925. The tune was naturally named THAXTED, after the Essex town which Holst had made his home, and in honour of the countryside that had first inspired him to create the great masterpiece from which the tune is taken.

Holst may have regretted recycling the music from *Jupiter* in this way. *The Planets* was an astonishing outpouring of originality and orchestral mastery; but when *I vow to thee, my country* started to gain popularity as a patriotic song, Holst complained that conductors began to perform that passage from *Jupiter* as if it were a hymn. Whatever his misgivings, THAXTED has rightly established itself as a deep-rooted favourite among hymn-singers, as much a part of Remembrance services as *Jerusalem* and the National Anthem.

❖

WE NEED TO HEAD WEST NOW. Our journey now takes us to the birthplace of a tune that is every bit as patriotic as JERUSALEM or THAXTED—though most people have forgotten this.

Chapter 7

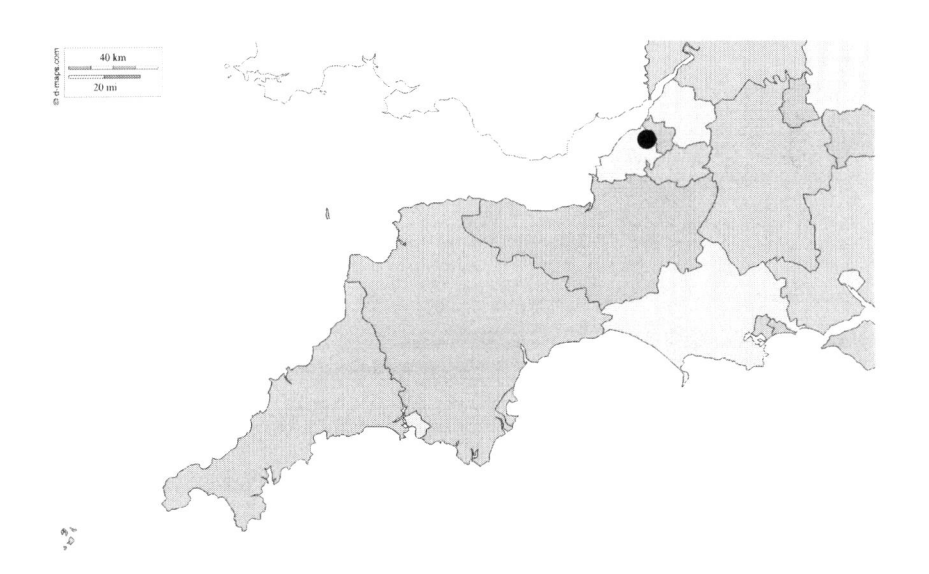

ABBOT'S LEIGH

Abbot's Leigh

Glorious things of thee are spoken

Glor-ious things of thee are spok-en, Zi-on, ci-ty of our God;

CYRIL VINCENT TAYLOR 1907-1991[1]

ABBOT'S LEIGH is a village a few miles to the west of Bristol. It was originally known simply as Leigh (or Lega)—a common element in English place-names, meaning a clearing. But in 1140 the lord of the manor, Robert Fitzharding, founded St Augustine's Abbey (which went on to become Bristol Cathedral), and Leigh subsequently adopted the prefix 'Abbot's'.

Leigh Court, the current manor house, was built in 1814, replacing an Elizabethan building which was demolished in 1812. By all accounts the original house was magnificent, and it is impossible to imagine its destruction being permitted today. The old Tudor manor house is famous for an incident which happened in 1651. One evening in September the then owner of the house, George Norton, was visited by a family friend called Jane Lane, who brought with her a male companion whom he did not know. Norton welcomed the travellers into his house. Mrs Norton was expecting a baby, and Jane Lane had seemingly come to pay her a visit, but while she was at Leigh Court Jane received a letter informing her that her father was seriously ill, so she and her companions left after a few days.

What George Norton did not know was that the unknown man who had turned up with Jane Lane was in fact the fugitive Charles II, fleeing in disguise after being defeated at the Battle of Worcester. Charles was

---

[1] ABBOT'S LEIGH by C V Taylor (1907-91) © Oxford University Press 1941. Extract reproduced by permission. All rights reserved.

recognised by one of Norton's servants, but managed to avoid detection by speaking to a soldier who had fought in the battle, asking him to describe the King's appearance and clothing. The soldier, guessing the ruse, replied 'The King was at least three inches taller than you.' Charles eventually managed to leave the country, landing in France on 16th October, having narrowly escaped the Parliamentarian forces on several occasions. After the Restoration, George Norton was knighted, perhaps as a gesture of thanks from the king he unwittingly protected.

Daily Service dilemmas

In somewhat more recent times, Abbot's Leigh was home to the Revd Cyril Vincent Taylor. Taylor was not a native of Somerset: he was born in Wigan in Lancashire in 1907. As a boy he was a chorister at Magdalen College, Oxford, and he went on to read Classics at Christ Church, after which he studied Theology in Cambridge. He was ordained in 1931, and went to work as Precentor and Sacristan of Bristol Cathedral in 1936. Later he was precentor at Salisbury Cathedral.

During his time at Bristol he also worked for the BBC. At the outbreak of war the BBC's religious broadcasting unit moved from London to Bristol, presumably to avoid being bombed. Taylor became responsible for the Daily Service, a programme that had been broadcast since 1928 and which continues to this day.

**Cyril Vincent Taylor
1907–1991**

One of Taylor's duties was to select the hymns that were to be included in the broadcast. In 1941 he found he had a problem. John Newton's hymn *Glorious things of thee are spoken* had been popular since its first appearance in 1779; indeed it remains popular now. The words are grand and poetic, and Taylor wanted to be able to use them in a broadcast. The problem was the tune.

At that time the tune to which *Glorious things* was sung was always the one known to hymn-books as AUSTRIA. It is a tune of great beauty by one of the greatest of all composers: so why did Taylor think there was a problem with it?

> **John Newton (1725–1807)** first went to sea aboard a merchant ship at the age of eleven. In 1743 he was pressed into the Royal Navy and became a midshipman. After having been flogged and demoted for attempted desertion, he transferred to a slave-ship. He was abandoned in West Africa and for a while was little more than a slave himself. In 1748 he was rescued and set sail for England in a merchant ship. On the voyage home the vessel suffered severe weather and was at risk of sinking. Waking in the night to find the ship filling with water, Newton prayed to God, whereupon the leak was sealed by a chance movement of the cargo, and the ship was saved. This marked the beginning of his conversion to evangelical Christianity, though he continued in the slave-trade for some time afterwards, and did not openly speak out against it for decades. He wrote many hymns, the best-known of which are *Amazing Grace* and *Glorious things of thee are spoken*.

God save the Emperor

The tune in question was not originally written for John Newton's words. It started life as a birthday present for a king.

The Emperor Francis II (1768-1835) was Holy Roman Emperor from 1792 to 1806. (After 1806 there were no more Holy Roman Emperors.) Despite the job-title, his realms were in Austria, Germany and Hungary, not Rome.

Francis and his family were highly cultured people. His younger brother, Rudolph, was a pupil and close friend of Beethoven, who dedicated many works to him including the *Archduke Trio* and his fifth piano concerto. (The title 'Emperor Concerto' was not given by Beethoven, and indeed is only used in the English-speaking world; it refers to the character of the music and has nothing to do with a specific Emperor, Holy Roman or otherwise.)

Francis too moved in the company of great composers—specifically Beethoven's own teacher, Haydn. In 1797, when Francis was 29, Haydn presented to him a song specially written for his birthday, called *Gott erhalte Franz den Kaiser* (God save the Emperor). It is possible that Haydn based the tune on a Croatian folk-song: there is certainly one such song whose first phrase is startlingly similar to Haydn's tune. However, the melody that we know is certainly by Haydn.

He was pleased with it. After using it in the Emperor's birthday song, Haydn recycled the tune in a number of works, the best-known of which is probably the slow movement of the String Quartet no. 62 in C major, opus 76 no. 3, familiarly known as the 'Emperor Quartet'. It is reported that this tune was the very last thing that Haydn played on the piano before he died.

Joseph Haydn
1732–1809

Haydn wasn't the only person to appreciate the tune, and it began to be re-used in all sorts of places. In England it was very quickly adopted as a hymn-tune. In 1800 it appeared in a book called *Sacred Music* by Edward Miller, and a few years later in 1809 it was printed in a collection called *Psalms, hymns and anthems for the Foundling Chapel*, set to the hymn *Praise the Lord, ye heavens adore him* (to which it is still often sung). It appeared in the Supplement to the second edition of *Hymns Ancient & Modern* in 1889, where it was called AUSTRIA and paired with *Glorious things of thee are spoken*.

What was so wrong with AUSTRIA?

String quartets and hymn-books were not the only ways in which Haydn's tune was being used. In 1841 a German writer called August Heinrich Hoffmann wrote a song using this tune called *Das Lied der Deutschen* (song of the Germans). At the time Germany was not a single country, but there were many who believed that it should be united into one nation. Hoffmann was one of these, and the lyrics he fitted to *Gott erhalte Franz den Kaiser* were a plea for integration of the various German states. The idea of Germany as an entity was, he argued, a higher ideal than any local or regional loyalty. Germany should come first: Germany, Germany above all.

Or as Hoffmann put it, *Deutschland, Deutschland über alles*.

These words are often misunderstood. They were not (at least to begin with) meant to be a boast of German supremacy over all other nations: they are a call for brotherly togetherness.

The *Lied der Deutschen* did not become the official German national anthem until 1922, long after its tune had been transplanted into English hymn-books. As far as I know no-one had any problem singing *Glorious things* to this tune all the way through the First World War. By the time of the Second World War, however, things were different. *Deutschland über alles* now really did seem to mean not just a united Germany but an all-powerful Germany that wanted to revive the Holy Roman Empire, and the later German empire, and forge a third empire—a third Reich— that would last a thousand years. Haydn's gentle, elegant happy birthday tune had become the marching-song for a terrifying, ruthless foe.

Cyril Taylor still admired John Newton's stirring words. But the tune they brought with them was now the enemy's national anthem, and it was very unlikely that the BBC would agree to broadcast it as part of an act of worship.

A home-grown melody

So, one Sunday in 1941, Taylor sat down and in the space of a single morning wrote a new tune, naming it ABBOT'S LEIGH after the village where he was living. It is a magnificent tune, which congregations love: a great one for ending a service with. As director of the Daily Service Taylor had a ready-made nationwide audience for his tune, and it soon became popular. At last people could sing *Glorious things of thee are spoken* again, without seeming unpatriotic.

In 1951 the BBC brought out its own hymn-book, of which Taylor was one of the editors; nineteen of the tunes in this book were by him, including of course ABBOT'S LEIGH. This helped seal its popularity, and today it is probably used for Newton's hymn more often than the Haydn tune.

Memorial in Salisbury Cathedral

The tune does have a pitfall for singers, though. In the very last phrase of the music, where the words for Verse 1 are *Thou may'st smile at all thy foes*, there is a big downward leap from 'all' to 'thy' which is not quite what you might expect. Avoiding the obvious is of course a mark of originality; but tunes for congregational singing have to be obvious enough to allow ordinary worshippers to pick up the melody after one or two hearings. Quite often inexperienced singers plump for a slightly smaller downward leap, resulting in a phrase which works perfectly well but is not what Taylor wrote.

In a brief biographical article about Taylor in the *Bulletin of the Hymn Society* Bernard Massey has this to say about ABBOT'S LEIGH:

> But in any event Abbot's Leigh, one of the great hymn-tunes of all time, will keep his name alive indefinitely—and when the trumpets

sounded for him on the other side they no doubt delighted him by playing its last line correctly.[2]

❖

SOON WE WILL BE HEADING BACK EAST, but before we do so, let's cross over the Bristol Channel for a brief foray into Wales, the Land of Song.

---

[2] Bernard S Massey, *Bulletin of the Hymn Society* 189, October 1991, pp. 69-71. Extract reproduced by permission.

Chapter 8

Cwm Rhondda

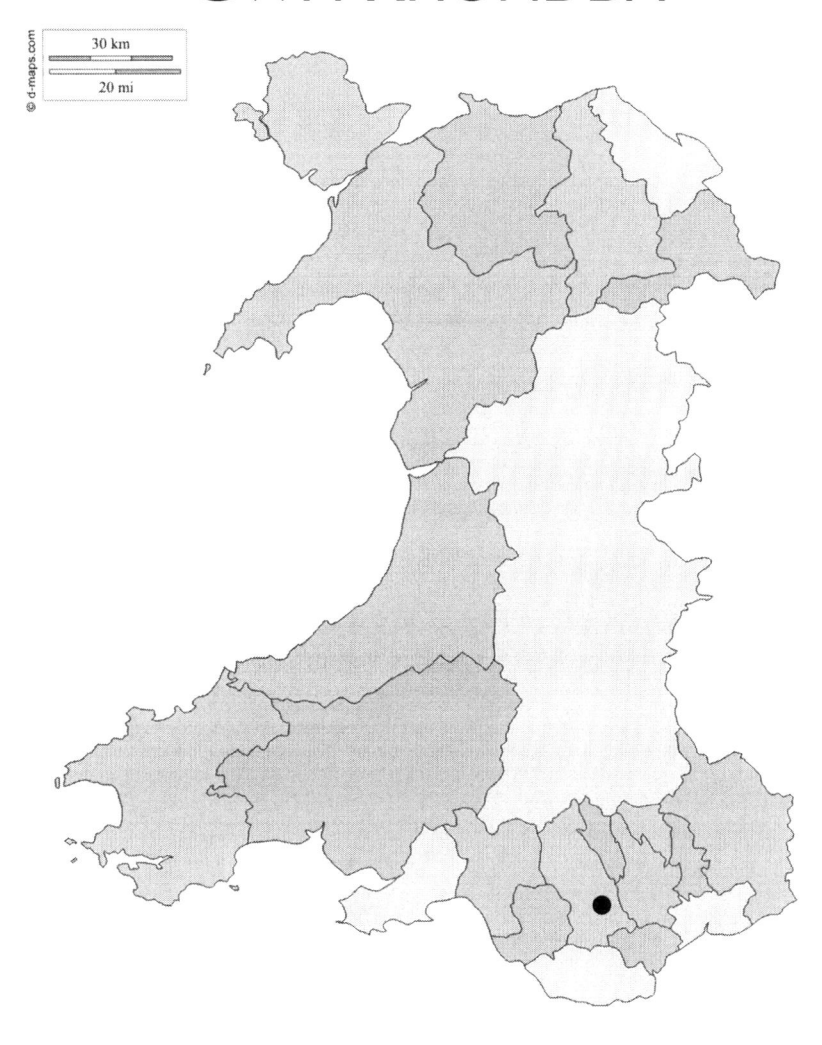

Cwm Rhondda

Guide me, O thou great Redeemer

Guide me, O thou great Re-deem-er, Pil-grim through this bar-ren land.

JOHN HUGHES 1873-1932

CWM RHONDDA simply means 'Rhondda Valley'. In fact there are two Rhondda valleys: the Rhondda Fawr (or Great Rhondda) and the Rhondda Fach (or Little Rhondda). They merge into a single Rhondda river at the village of Porth, about three miles west of Pontypridd. The origin of the name Rhondda is uncertain: according to one theory, it comes from an old word *rhawdd*, related to modern Welsh *adrawdd*, to relate or recite, and the Old Welsh adjective *gnou*, renowned. It seems to refer to the idea that the river speaks (much as we refer to babbling brooks). The name has been through various metamorphoses, including Rhoddeni and Glynroddney, before settling down to its modern spelling.

Throughout history the beauty of these valleys has been charming travellers who were lucky enough to behold them. In 1803 B H Malkin described the Rhondda as the 'Alps of Glamorgan'; while Charles Cliffe, writing in 1847, maintained that this region was the 'gem of South Wales and hardly surpassed through the Alpine North'. In her book *The Matter of Wales* Jan Morris quotes (but does not name) a writer of the 1840s: 'The people of this solitudinous and happy valley are a pastoral race, almost entirely dependent on their flocks and herds for support.'

But only a few years after these words were written, the landscape and character of the Rhondda had changed radically by the arrival of the coal industry.

In 1851 John Calvert, a Yorkshireman, opened the Gyfellion Pit at Hopkinstown, in Pontypridd, not far from where the two Rhondda valleys come together. This mine later came under the ownership of the Great Western Colliery Company, and by the 1890s it employed around 1,400 men. In April 1893 a young lad who worked at the Great Western went down the mine-shaft to start his afternoon shift. On his way he saw flames underneath a haulage engine, part of the machinery for moving the coal up to the surface. The engine was fitted with wooden brake-blocks which heated up due to friction when they were deployed. The man who usually worked this particular engine was in the habit of cooling the brakes with water; but he had been off sick for some days and his replacement had not been warned to do this. A spark from the hot brake-blocks seems to have caused the wooden frame on which the engine was fixed to catch fire. The flames quickly spread, filling the pit with thick smoke.

Sixty-three men and boys died in the Great Western Colliery fire. It was a shocking disaster, but by no means unique: in the century or so that followed the arrival of coal-mining, fatal accidents were almost commonplace, and in many cases the death-toll of a single disaster was over one hundred. Coal brought prosperity to the mine owners and employment to thousands, but it came at a great personal cost to the families who depended on it.

The land of song

The Welsh have always taken music and poetry seriously. The earliest eisteddfod was probably held in the Middle Ages: a gathering of musicians and poets called to perform for the lord of the castle, with the prize of a seat at the high table being bestowed on the best performer. The word *eisteddfod* literally means 'sitting down'—a reference to the chair or throne awarded to the winner. By Tudor times the contests had become formalised and indeed regulated. By order of Queen Elizabeth I, the bards had to undergo an examination in order to gain the right to take part; if successful, they were literally granted a poetic licence.

In the following centuries the tradition of the eisteddfod waned, until a poet named Edward Williams (1747–1826) began a revival that led to the National Eisteddfod which flourishes to this day. Williams— better known by his bardic name of Iolo Morganwg—was a writer who published editions of medieval Welsh literature; where there were gaps in the body of available manuscripts, he shamelessly plugged them with his own forgeries. Among his notable achievements was the 'discovery' of an ancient runic alphabet, known as the *Coelbren y Beirdd*, that had been used by the druids; he managed to convince many people of the authenticity of this alphabet, and in 1838 his son Taliesin Williams was awarded a prize at the Abergavenny Eisteddfod for showing that it was genuine. Of course, the whole thing had been invented by Edward Williams.

In 1792 Williams organised what he called the *Gorsedd y Beirdd Ynys Prydain*, the Throne of the Bards of the Isle of Britain. It was his attempt to breathe new life into the flagging tradition of the eisteddfod. To further this aim he 'discovered' a whole liturgy of druidic ritual and ceremony, as authentic as his runic alphabet. The first eisteddfod of Williams' revival, held on the day of the autumnal equinox, was held, oddly, in Primrose Hill in London, the very place from which, just over a century later, Percy Dearmer would launch *The English Hymnal*. This spawned rival gatherings in Wales, and by 1860 the movement had produced the National Eisteddfod in more or less its current form.

Welsh hymns

What of hymns? How does the Welsh love of song and verse manifest itself in church or chapel? The eisteddfod and the bardic tradition are not primarily religious in nature, though they are saturated with ritual and ceremony. The Welsh have always liked to walk their own path when it comes to religion. In the earliest days of Christianity in Britain, the Celtic Church followed its own way, reluctant to be brought into line by the mainstream Catholic orthodoxy. After the Reformation and Henry VIII's break from Rome, the new faith of the Church of England was imposed by law; but it seems that—perhaps unsurprisingly—the Welsh never really took it to their hearts. The folk-culture of the Welsh has always preferred to look back, like Iolo Morganwg, to a pre-Christian era—real, imagined, or half-remembered. Their legends are full of references to the *Tylwyth Teg*: noble creatures of the otherworld, fair to behold but dangerous to meet, whose lordly bearing is somewhat reminiscent of the Elves of Middle-Earth (indeed, the language spoken by most of Tolkien's Elves was deliberately designed to look and sound like Welsh). So it is perhaps not surprising that hymns and hymn-books were for many years relatively rare in the land of song.

The Tudor Book of Common Prayer was translated into Welsh in 1567 by the scholar William Salesbury (1520–1581) and the Bishop of St David's, Richard Davies (1505–1581). The first complete Welsh Bible came in 1588, by William Morgan (1545-1604), Bishop of Llandaff and of St Asaph. But it was not until 1621 that the first comprehensive collection of metrical psalms was published: *Llyfr y Psalmau*, by Edmwnd Prys (1542/3-1623), probably with help from William Morgan. Whereas the English equivalents such as Sternhold & Hopkins tended to use Common Metre, most of the hymns in Prys's book were in what came to be known as *Mesur Salm* or Psalm Metre. The basic form of this type of verse is a four-line stanza, with eight syllables in lines 1 and 3, alternating with seven syllables in lines 2 and 4. Sometimes this was doubled, to give an eight-line stanza in 8.7.8.7.8.7.8.7 metre. An English example of double *Mesur Salm* would be:

> *Glorious things of thee are spoken,*
> *Zion, city of our God*
> *He whose word cannot be broken*
> *Formed thee for his own abode.*
> *On the rock of ages founded,*

What can shake thy sure repose?
With salvation's walls surrounded,
Thou may'st smile at all thy foes.

This metre is particularly suited to Welsh poetry, because it gives a lot of scope for so-called 'feminine' endings, where the last syllable is unstressed—a common occurrence in Welsh.

Edmwnd Prys's book had very few important successors in the seventeenth century. The real flowering of Welsh hymnody had to wait for a development within the Church that would strike a chord with the national reluctance to conform. It was only with the coming of Methodism that the Welsh found a version of Christianity that they could truly reconcile with their centuries-old passion for song.

The Revival

The founder of the Methodist movement, John Wesley, was suspicious of the Welsh, whom he described as 'pagan as Red Indians'. Nevertheless, the movement he founded, which preached good news to the poor and deliverance for the captive, spread quickly among the Welsh, who had for centuries been under the political shadow of their much larger neighbour. Wesley's principal apostle in Wales was Hywel (or Howell) Harris (1714–1773). Harris had a profound spiritual experience at Pentecost in 1735 which spurred him to spread the word throughout south Wales, establishing a form of worship that proved popular and enduring. The Methodist Revival—known in Welsh as *Y Diwygiad*—lit a fire in the souls of the people which the official creeds of Catholicism and Anglicanism had never even come close to. Preachers would stir up their congregations with a passion that was perhaps not always wholly spiritual. Harris himself was never officially received into the Methodist fold, and for much of his life was at odds with the Wesleys. His relationship with a married woman named Madam Griffith, who claimed to be able to foretell the future, raised some eyebrows; and even one of Harris's own converts, the poet and hymn-writer William Williams Pantycelyn, commented wryly on the way that the Revival preachers strayed dangerously close to the all-too-narrow border between the sacred and the carnal: 'the flesh also insisted on having its share, and all the passions of nature aroused by grace were rioting tumultuously'.

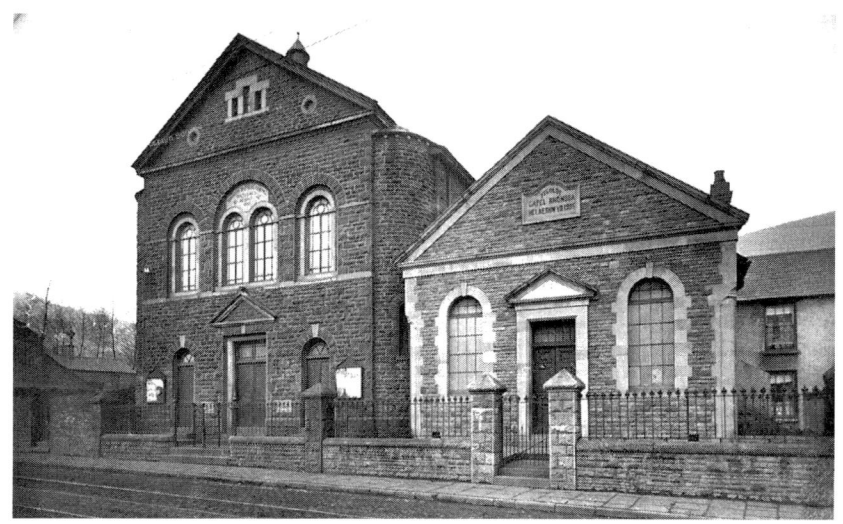

Capel Rhondda Welsh Baptist Chapel in Hopkinstown, Pontypridd
Used by kind permission of Rhondda Cynon Taff Libraries

It was the Methodists, and other Nonconformists such as the Baptists, who really made the link between Welsh song and Welsh religion, and gave us the strong tradition of Welsh hymns that includes not only the poetry of Williams and his successors, but great tunes like BLAENWERN, HYFRYDOL and CWM RHONDDA.

> **William Williams (1717–1791)**, often known as 'Pantycelyn' after the farm in Carmarthenshire where he lived, was probably the greatest of Welsh hymn-writers. In 1740 he heard Hywel Harris preaching in Talgarth near the River Wye, the very place where Harris himself had had his defining Pentecostal moment. Williams was stirred up by the message he heard and joined the Methodist movement. He was ordained deacon in the established church but fell foul of the authorities for preaching outside the parish, and never became a priest.
>
> In 1744 he published *Aleluia*, a collection of hymns. He expanded this over the next few years with new verses, including some by other writers. Then in 1762 he brought out *Caniadau y rhai sydd ar y Môr o Wydr* (The Songs of those upon the Sea of Glass). This collection included the hymn *Arglwydd, arwain trwy'r anialwch*, which was later translated by Peter Williams (1723–1796) as *Guide me, O thou great Jehovah*.
>
> The Methodists placed much emphasis on the singing of hymns as part of collective worship, and just as the Wesleys reinvigorated English hymnody, so Williams brought new life to Welsh hymns. Although he was a native Welsh speaker, all his formal education had been in English. This meant that his use of Welsh was not scholarly, and even suffered from formal errors; but it did enable him to experiment with new metres and bring a freshness to his poetry that other writers lacked.

The writing of Cwm Rhondda

The Capel Rhondda Welsh Baptist Chapel in Hopkinstown was originally opened in 1853 and rebuilt in 1885. In 1907 a new pipe-organ was installed, and the organist and precentor, D W Thomas, decided that a new hymn-tune should be commissioned to mark the inauguration of the instrument. He asked John Hughes, the clerk at the Great

Western Colliery, if he would provide the music. Hughes was born in 1873 and from the age of twelve he had worked in the coal industry, first at Glynn Colliery at Llanilltud Faerdref near Pontypridd, and then from 1905 at the Great Western in Hopkinstown, the site of the 1893 disaster. He was talented musician, serving as precentor and deacon at the Salem Baptist Chapel.

It was a few weeks before Hughes got the inspiration for the new tune. Then one Sunday he came back home after the morning service and said to his wife, 'I think I have it.' He went to the piano and started working out his ideas, spending the rest of the day composing the tune and even skipping the other chapel services in order to finish the job.

On 1st November 1907 the tune had its first performance in the Capel Rhondda chapel, with Hughes himself playing the new organ. The words were a hymn by Ann Griffiths (1776–1805), *Wele'n sefyll rhwng y myrtwydd* ('Lo, between the myrtles standing'). Griffiths was brought up as an Anglican but joined the Methodists in 1796. During her short life (she died in childbirth at the age of 29) she composed a small number of Welsh verses, of which *Wele'n sefyll rhwng y myrtwydd* is the best known because of its association with Hughes' tune. These are still the words that are most commonly sung to this tune in Wales.

Initially the tune was simply known as RHONDDA; it was the conductor Harry Evans (1873–1914) who renamed it CWM RHONDDA to help distinguish it from another tune of the same name. For many years Hughes resisted publishing it in a book: it was only available as a leaflet, with standard music notation on one side and tonic sol-fa on the other. But in 1918 it was included in a book called *Cân a Mawl* (Song and Praise), a collection of hymns in both Welsh and English published in Chicago, in which it was paired with the Christmas carol *Angels from the realms of glory*.

Did anybody say Jehovah?

It was not until 1920 that CWM RHONDDA became associated with William Williams' hymn *Arglwydd, arwain trwy'r anialwch*—or rather, the English translation by Peter Williams, *Guide me, O thou great Jehovah*: the Welsh version of this hymn is still usually sung to a different tune.

And yes, the earliest English version does use 'Jehovah'. The change to 'Redeemer' occurred in 1861 when the hymn was included in *Hymns Ancient & Modern*; ever since then, editors of hymn-books have had to make a choice between the two possibilities. The Welsh is no help here: *Arglwydd* simply means 'lord'. The name of Jehovah recalls the Old Testament imagery of the hymn, with its echoes of the Exodus: the use of 'Redeemer' provides a link back to the New Testament. Many English hymn-books have plumped for the latter, including *The English Hymnal* and *Common Praise*.

While we're on the subject of the translation, it is interesting to note that the Welsh hymn does not make any direct reference to 'bread of Heaven': at that point in the first verse it simply says '*Hollalluog, hollalluog*' ('Almighty, Almighty'). Verse three does, however, contain the phrase '*Rho i mi fanna*' ('Give me manna').

From the 1930s onwards CWM RHONDDA was regularly included in hymn-books. It has become well-known in church and chapel, and has also taken on a life outside formal worship. Perhaps one of the most familiar of hymn-tunes, its greatness lies in its ability to carry Williams' Old Testament imagery with dignity, as well as being belted out with gusto on the terraces at rugby matches.

❖

NEXT WE ARE TRAVELLING back to England, to visit the birthplace of a man responsible for some of the finest hymn-tunes of all.

Chapter 9

Down Ampney

DOWN AMPNEY

Come down, O Love divine

Come down, O Love div - ine, seek thou this soul of mine,

RALPH VAUGHAN WILLIAMS 1872-1958[1]

OWN AMPNEY IS MENTIONED in the Domesday Book, where it is called Amenel and is recorded as having 35 households. Domesday also tells us that in 1066, just before the Conquest, its lord was someone with the enviable name of Ednoth the Constable. The prefix 'Down' seems to have been acquired later, as was the 'p' in Ampney. Older people from the area still pronounce the name 'Amney' but the 'p' is beginning to make itself heard, especially in the speech of newcomers.

Down Ampney is in Gloucestershire: a Cotswold village of honey-coloured stone, with a spired church but, as far as I can find, no pub. During the Second World War there was an airfield nearby which played an important part in both Operation Market Garden (Arnhem) and the D-Day invasions in 1944. The church has a stained glass window commemorating the village's involvement in these events, and each year in September a special Arnhem Service is held.

The village is also important as the birthplace of one of the greatest of English composers.

In 1868 a new vicar named Arthur Vaughan Williams moved into Down Ampney vicarage, fresh from his honeymoon. As you might guess from his name, the vicar's ancestry was partly Welsh; but he had grown up in Surrey on the slopes of Leith Hill, where his father, a senior judge,

---

[1] DOWN AMPNEY by Ralph Vaughan Williams (1872-1958) from *The English Hymnal*. Extract reproduced by permission of Oxford University Press. All rights reserved.

had rented a house. It was in the neighbourhood of Leith Hill that he had met his bride, Margaret Wedgwood.

Margaret came from a very eminent and interesting family. Her childhood home was Leith Hill Place, which had been bought in 1847 by her father, Josiah Wedgwood III, grandson of the famous potter. Josiah had married his cousin Caroline Darwin; what's more, his sister Emma Wedgwood had married Caroline's brother, Charles Darwin. The great naturalist and author of *The Origin of Species* was therefore Margaret Wedgwood's uncle. He was very affectionate towards her and her two sisters, addressing them as My Dear Angels and getting them to help with his research into earthworms and his botanical investigations.

> **Ralph Vaughan Williams** (1872–1958) was one of the foremost English composers of the first half of the twentieth century. He was educated at Charterhouse School, Trinity College Cambridge, and the Royal College of Music, where his tutors included Charles Villiers Stanford and Charles Hubert Hastings Parry. He also studied with Max Bruch (1838–1920) in Berlin and Maurice Ravel (1875–1937) in Paris.
>
> In 1914 he enlisted as a private in the Royal Ambulance Medical Corps, even though his education and social class would have entitled him to an officer's commission.
>
> During his long life Vaughan Williams produced a vast quantity of music, including nine symphonies, operas, concertos, choral works, songs, chamber music, ballet—and, of course, hymns. He was one of the first major composers to compose music for the cinema, including the score for the 1948 film *Scott of the Antarctic*, which he later reshaped into his seventh symphony, *Sinfonia Antartica*. His ashes are buried in Westminster Abbey.

Margaret and her husband had three children while they were living in the vicarage at Down Ampney. The youngest, Ralph—whose first name, by the way, is pronounced *Rafe*—was born there on 12 October 1872.

The Old Vicarage, Down Ampney

Ralph Vaughan Williams did not live in Down Ampney for long, but clearly held it in some affection, because many years later he used the name for one of the most beautiful hymn-tunes in the repertoire. But why was the great composer dabbling in hymns in the first place?

The parson who invited tramps into his drawing-room

In 1904, when Vaughan Williams was living in London, he had an unexpected visit:

> I was sitting in my study in Barton Street, Westminster, when a hansom drove up to the door and Mr Dearmer was announced. I just knew his name vaguely as a parson who invited tramps to sleep in his drawing room, and I wondered if he was going to ask me to do the same.

But Percy Dearmer had not come looking for accommodation for his tramps. Instead he wanted to talk to Vaughan Williams about a new hymn-book that he was planning. He and a group of other clerics and interested laymen found themselves dissatisfied with the mawkish sentimentality, bad verse and dull music found in the old Victorian hymnbooks such as *Hymns Ancient & Modern*, and were determined to do something better. He had come to ask Vaughan Williams to be the music editor.

It was perhaps a strange choice. Vaughan Williams was not really a church musician, though he had taken a job as organist while he was studying at the Royal College of Music in the 1890s. Nor was he even a church-goer. When he was at Trinity College, Cambridge, it was compulsory for undergraduates to attend Chapel, but he did not always comply wholeheartedly. One morning he was summoned to explain his absence:

> 'I did not see you in Chapel this morning, Mr Vaughan Williams.'
> 'No, Sir.'
> 'Perhaps, however, you were in the organ loft?'
> 'Yes, Sir, I was.'
> 'Well, you can pray as well in the organ loft as in any other part of the Chapel.'
> 'Yes, Sir—but I didn't.'

It was Cecil Sharp who had put forward Vaughan Williams' name to Percy Dearmer. He was on the point of refusing, but Dearmer mentioned that his second choice for music editor was Henry Walford Davies, whom Vaughan Williams described as 'a well-known Church musician with whose musical ideas I was much out of sympathy.' Having thought it over for twenty-four hours, he accepted the job.

> **Percy Dearmer** (1867-1936) was the vicar of the Parish Church of St Mary the Virgin in Primrose Hill from 1901 to 1916. As well as being the original Editor of *The English Hymnal*, he was author of *The Parson's Handbook*, a hugely influential book which sought to address—and redress—some of the problems Dearmer perceived in the Church of England of his day. Many of Vaughan Williams's hymn-tunes, including MONKS GATE and DOWN AMPNEY, were first sung by Dearmer's congregation at St Mary's.

The English Hymnal

Percy Dearmer's hymn-book became *The English Hymnal*. Today it is a classic among hymn collections, as much a part of the establishment as *Hymns Ancient & Modern*. I grew up with it: when I was a child I thought it was *the* hymnbook, and loved looking through the bits of the book that weren't just the words to hymns, marvelling in delight and incomprehension at the index of original first lines that included such mysteries as ᾌσωμεν πάντες λαοί. But when it was first published *The English Hymnal* caused consternation in the Church, mainly because of the inclusion of hymns with a supposedly Catholic whiff—rather too much mention of Our Lady for some tastes. It has survived as a hymn book, largely because of the quality of the verse (some of it commissioned specially by Dearmer from such eminent poets as Robert Bridges and G K Chesterton)—and, of course, the music.

O Little Town

Vaughan Williams' vision for the hymnal was that 'besides being a compendium of all the tunes of worth that were already in use, the book should, in addition, be a thesaurus of all the finest hymn tunes in the world.' To this end he more than once persuaded Dearmer and his colleagues to write new words to fit old tunes that he thought worthy of preservation: this was the origin of that great hymn *Ye watchers and ye holy ones*, with words by Athelstan Riley to music that RVW adapted from a German Easter hymn. In *The English Hymnal* this tune is called Lasst uns erfreuen, and elsewhere I have seen it called simply Easter Hymn, neither of which are place-names, so unfortunately it falls outside the scope of my current journey.

The process worked the other way. Dearmer often came up with poems that he thought would make good hymns, or words that were already hymns but with dreary tunes, and Vaughan Williams had to supply the music. To find tunes, he often turned to the music of the land, the folk-songs he had collected in his travels in recent years, making a few adjustments here and there to make the tunes fit better, just as the folk-singers themselves had done. He also trawled ancient sources from both this country and abroad, resurrecting old German chorales and even older plainsong melodies.

Few of the hymn-tunes that Vaughan Williams supplied for *The English Hymnal* were his own original compositions. He rather disapproved of the prolific tune-writing that had gone on during the Victorian era. Percy Scholes, writing in *The Oxford Companion to Music*, put forward the opinion that there was no need for any new hymn-tunes, and suggested that no one should even try to compose one 'unless they are sure of the possession of very special gifts'. I think Vaughan Williams might well have agreed with him.

Fine tunes

Nevertheless, Vaughan Williams—who did possess *very* special gifts—composed a handful of new tunes for the new hymn-book. At least three of these have become established classics. SALVE FESTA DIES (sung to *Hail thee, festival day* and *Christians lift up your hearts*), is a jolly good sing once you've got the hang of it, but it's a bit quirky, with a different tune for odd and even verses and another one for the chorus. The tune he wrote to go with *For all the saints* is one you can really throw yourself into, and is possibly my favourite hymn-tune of all. He called it SINE NOMINE, which is Latin for 'without a name'. This may be a reference to the fact that in early editions of the *Hymnal* he was not credited as composer; or it may simply be that he couldn't think of a name.

But perhaps the best-known of the tunes that Vaughan Williams composed for the new book was the one he named after his birthplace, DOWN AMPNEY.

The words for this hymn, *Come down, O Love divine*, are a translation of an Italian hymn called *Discendi, amor santo* by Bianco da Siena, a woolcomber turned monk who lived in Italy in the fourteenth century. The original begins as follows:

> *Discendi, amor santo,*
> *Visita la mia mente*
> *Del tuo amore ardente,*
> *Si che di te m'infiammi tutto quanto.*

This poem was freely adapted and translated into English by Richard Frederick Littledale (1833-1890), an Irish-born clergyman. He published his translation in a book called *The People's Hymnal*, which he brought out in 1867. There it stayed in comparative obscurity until it was brought to the attention of the editors of *The English Hymnal*, and Vaughan Williams was asked to provide a tune for it. I do not know if he tried to fit it to an existing tune before composing his own: if he did try, it is fortunate that he did not succeed. DOWN AMPNEY is one of the glories of hymnody. No doubt the choice of name for this tune was partly suggested by the words of the hymn (*Come* DOWN, *O Love divine*). But I like to think that by giving it the name of his idyllic birthplace Vaughan Williams was investing the tune with a very personal significance—much more than the anonymity of SINE NOMINE.

❖

FINE TUNES INDEED. But perhaps Vaughan Williams' greatest contribution to hymn-music was the many tunes he adapted from folk-songs. Some of these have become so familiar to us that their earthy origins are all but forgotten. One such is the tune that goes with the carol from which this book takes its title; but before we go there, we must pay a visit to a pub just a few miles from where I live.

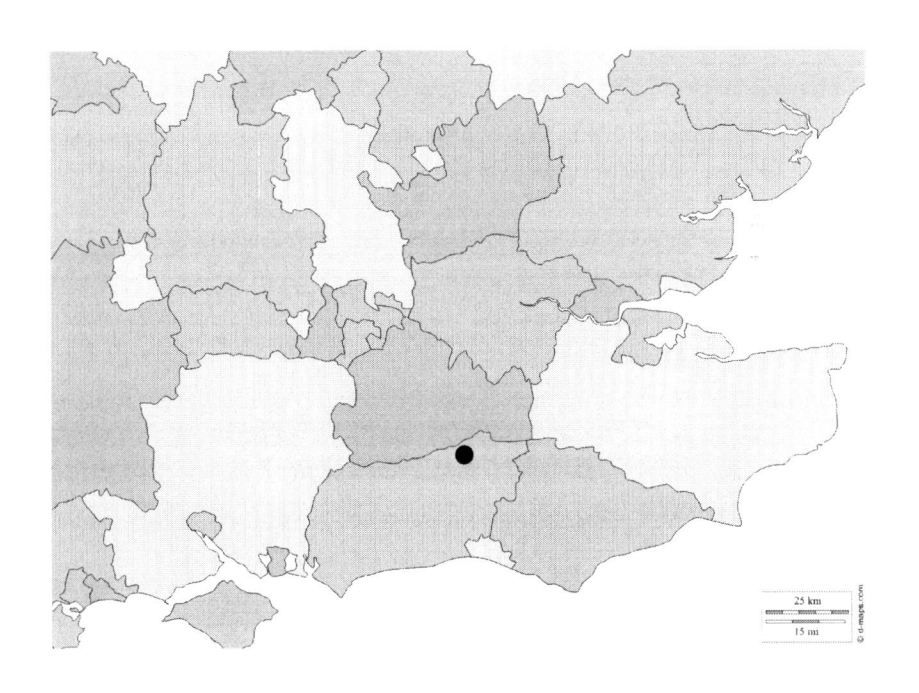

Chapter 10
KINGSFOLD

KINGSFOLD

I heard the voice of Jesus say

I heard the voice of Jes-us say, 'Come un-to me and rest;

MELODY FROM AN ENGLISH FOLKSONG

KINGSFOLD IS A HAMLET in the Parish of Warnham in West Sussex. The 'fold' element of the name means a clearing made in the woods to create space for farmland. Which king, if any, gave Kingsfold its royal-sounding name, I have not been able to discover. The earliest references to the name seem to be from the thirteenth century, when a family called Kingsfold held land in this area. Whether they took their name from the place or the other way round is not clear.

At that time, around 1250, there was no village or even hamlet called Kingsfold. It seems to have grown up very slowly over the centuries: even in Victorian times there were only a handful of houses there.

Today it is a thriving little community with its own identity, straddling the busy A24. There is a fine pub there called The Owl, which serves excellent food. A few years ago this pub was called The Wise Old Owl, and its inn-sign showed a creature that bore a disturbing resemblance to the late Alan Whicker. Fortunately that has now been replaced with a much more elegant fowl. Even further back the pub was run as a nightclub called Cromwell's, of which I have heard nothing good. But the original name of the inn, by which it was known from at least 1787, was The Wheatsheaf.

Just before Christmas, on 23rd December 1904, Ralph Vaughan Williams was in The Wheatsheaf in Kingsfold, listening to the locals singing their folk-songs. Then aged 32, he was not yet the huge untidy ramshackle colossus of English music that he later became: he was a tall young man of striking good looks just beginning to make his name in the musical world. Little more than a year earlier, in December 1903, he had collected his first folk-song, *Bushes and Briars*, from a Mr Pottipher of Brentwood in Essex; when he heard it, we are told, he felt it was something he had known all his life. This was only a few months later than the moment Cecil Sharp had begun collecting and preserving folk-songs after hearing *The Seeds of Love* sung by a gardener.

Vaughan Williams became an enthusiastic collector of folk-songs, sometimes inviting people to his home in Leith Hill but more often travelling through the countryside and hearing the songs sung in the places they belonged. Pubs were a good source of material, presumably because the locals could be induced to sing more readily if they had been bought a drink. The song that Vaughan Williams heard in the Wheatsheaf, sung by a Mr Booker, was called *The Ballad of Maria Martin*, and it told the story of events that occurred nearly eighty years earlier.

The Owl at Kingsfold (formerly The Wheatsheaf)

The murder in the Red Barn

In May 1827 Maria Marten, a young woman of 25 from Polstead in Suffolk, put on a brown coat, a striped waistcoat and blue trousers and went with her lover William Corder to a place known as the Red Barn, half a mile from her home. Corder was not Maria's first lover: she had a young son, Henry, by a previous acquaintance. She had also had a child by Corder who had not survived beyond infancy and had been buried unofficially by Corder. They planned to elope to Ipswich, and Corder promised Maria's stepmother, Ann Marten, that they would marry the very next day. Maria's disguise was needed, said Corder, because the local constable had a warrant to take Maria and prosecute her for having bastard children.

Ann Marten and her husband Thomas (Maria's father) saw Corder from time to time during the following weeks, but unfortunately Maria was never able to come with him; nor was she able to write, because of a bad hand.

In October Thomas received a letter from William Corder, dated from London, in which he wrote to say that he and Maria were now happily married, and settled in Newport on the Isle of Wight, where they hoped to find a farm 'whereby we can gain a livelihood', after which they would be able to look after little Henry. Corder also mentioned that Maria had sent a letter to her father some time earlier, describing the wedding, 'and we feel astonished that you have not answered it, thinking illness must have been the cause.'

There are some little details in the letter that give us an idea of the young couple's new life on the island. William mentions happily that provisions are cheaper there than in the rest of England, and also reports that he and Maria have been taking advantage of their maritime surroundings:

'We have both been a great deal on the water, and have had some good sea-sicknesses, which I consider have been very useful to us both. My cough I lost entirely, which is a great consolation.'

Thomas and Ann Marten must have found this letter very consoling, as they had not seen Maria since May. But in the following months the cosy picture painted by this and other letters began to fade. There was no sign of Maria herself, and letters from her that William mentioned never seemed to arrive. Then Ann started having nightmares.

In these vivid dreams, Maria was not living happily in Newport, or indeed anywhere else, but lying dead in the Red Barn where she and William had hidden when they first set out from Polstead back in May of the previous year.

Eventually Ann became so troubled by the dreams that she persuaded her husband to search the barn. There he found a place where the earth had been disturbed. Digging down under this place, he found a dead body. The body had been there for nearly a year, but it was still recognisable as Maria's: the clothes were hers, and there were two teeth missing exactly where Maria was known to have gaps; there was also an identifiable wen on her neck. Around the neck of the corpse was William Corder's green handkerchief. There were also shot-wounds and she seemed to have been stabbed through the eye.

William Corder was tracked down to a boarding house in Brentford, where he was found boiling some eggs for breakfast in the company of some ladies. He was arrested and taken back to Suffolk, where he was tried in Bury St Edmunds.

Corder pleaded not guilty to the murder of Maria Marten. He claimed that he and Maria had quarrelled in the Red Barn and that she had unfavourably compared him to the other gentleman with whom she had had an affair, the father of little Henry. William had taken umbrage at this and threatened not to go through with the wedding. He went off in a huff but then was shocked to hear the sound of a gun going off. Running back to Maria he found her lifeless on the ground. To his horror he also found that the weapon she had used to kill herself was his own, which she had taken from his room some days earlier.

He at once saw that things looked bad for him. There were no witnesses, the death was clearly caused by one of his guns, and fingerprinting hadn't yet been invented. So in the hope of keeping out of trouble he buried Maria's body and tried to explain her disappearance by inventing a whole fictional married life on the Isle of Wight. The stab-wounds on the body were, he supposed, caused when Thomas Marten dug up the earth in the Red Barn with a pick.

The jury were not convinced by Corder's explanation. They took only thirty-five minutes to return with a verdict of guilty. He was sentenced to death by hanging, and executed on 11 August 1828. The night before his death he confessed he had killed her, though he claimed it was an accident during a quarrel about where their baby had been buried.

The Ballad of Maria Martin

The story of the murder in the Red Barn was an instant *cause célèbre*. It had all the elements of a cracking good yarn: sex, violence and mystery. You can imagine Holmes or Poirot tackling it, or Jonathan Creek explaining away the apparently supernatural mystery of Ann Marten's dreams. Even while the trial was in progress there were dramatic representations of the events, and afterwards there was a market in relics: locks of Maria's hair, pieces of the rope with which William Corder had been hanged, even portions of his body. The jury may have been clear about their verdict, but popular culture relished a number of alternative explanations. Perhaps Corder's version of the story was true. Or perhaps he and Ann Marten were having an affair.

There was no Poirot in those days, let alone Jonathan Creek, and even Sherlock Holmes would not appear for another sixty years. There were no tabloids; but plays, broadsides and ballads abounded. One such ballad—the one that Mr Booker sang to Vaughan Williams—runs as follows[1]:

>Come, all you thoughtless young men, a warning take by me,
>And think of my unhappy fate to be hanged upon a tree.
>My name is William Corder, to you I do declare,
>I courted Maria Martin, most beautiful and fair.
>
>I promised I would marry her upon a certain day.
>Instead of that I was resolved to take her life away.
>I went unto her father's house the 18th day of May.
>come, my dear Maria, and let us fix the day.
>
>If you will meet me at the Red Barn, as sure as I have life,
>I will take you to Ipswich town and there make you my wife.
>I straight went home and fetched my gun, my pickaxe and my spade,
>I went into the Red Barn, and there I dug her grave.
>
>With heart so light, she thought no harm, to meet me she did go.
>He murdered her all in the barn, and laid her body low.
>The horrid deed that he had done, she lay bleeding in her gore.
>Her bleeding and mangled body he threw on the Red Barn floor.
>
>Now, all things being silent, she could not take no rest,
>She appeared in her mother's house, who suckled her at her breast.
>For many a long month or more, her mind being sorely oppressed,
>Neither night nor day she could take no rest.
>
>Her mother's night being so disturbed she dreamt three nights o'er,
>Her daughter she lay murdered all on the Red Barn floor.

---

[1] The ballad spells Maria's surname 'Martin' but the original spelling is 'Marten'.

She sent her father to the barn, when in the ground he thrust.
And there he found his daughter, mingling with the dust.

My trial is hard, I could not stand, most woeful was the sight,
When her jaw-bone was brought to prove, which pierced me to the heart.
His aged mother standing by, likewise his loving wife,
And with her grief her hair she tore, she scarcely could keep life.

Adieu, adieu, my loving friends, my glass is almost run,
On Monday next, will be my last, when I am to be hung.
So you young men that do pass by, with pity look on me,
For murdering Maria Martin I was hanged upon a tree.

The first line of this ballad echoes a hundred folk-songs. Fans of the film *Master and Commander* will recall one called *The British Tars* that begins with almost exactly the same words:

Come all you bold young thoughtless men, a warning take by me
And never leave your happy homes to sail the raging seas.

It is a standard formula that can be applied to any situation. I have yet to discover whether or not *The British Tars* is older than *Maria Martin*; but the words 'Come all you...' crop up in countless songs on all sorts of subjects. Variants of this formula are found even in songs composed in more recent times: one of Bob Dylan's most famous lyrics starts 'Come gather 'round people, wherever you roam...' It is simply one of the ways of beginning a story, like 'Once upon a time' or 'There was an old man'. The opening of one old folk-carol runs as follows:

Come all ye faithful Christians,
That dwell within this land,
Don't spend your time in rioting,
Recollect you are but a man.

O Little Town

Be watchful of your latter end,
Be ready when you're called,
There's many changes in this world,
Some rise and some do fall.

In the second verse of this carol we are encouraged to remember the sufferings of Job, while verse three recalls the parable of the rich man and Lazarus. This rich man (traditionally known as Dives, which is nothing but the Latin for 'rich man') led a life of luxury, while poor Lazarus, all covered with sores, languished outside hoping to catch the crumbs that fell from the rich man's table. When they died, Lazarus was carried away by the angels to Abraham's bosom but Dives was cast in torment into Hades.

It's not the most cheery subject for a Christmas carol. But it is important to our story.

A very old tune

When Cecil Sharp and his collaborators reviewed their collections of folk-songs they found that the words and melodies were fluid and changeable. Passed on from singer to singer, the songs would evolve and adapt (like Darwin's beetles). The words and the music would separate, and in this game of *One Song to the Tune of Another* the singers often changed either the words or the melody so they fitted better. Sharp heard *Come all ye faithful Christians* sung by Mr John Dingle in Lew Trenchard, Devon, in 1904. The music that Mr Dingle sang was an adaptation, an evolution, of a very old tune.

The *Journal of the Folk-Song Society*, Volume II (1905-06), devotes a few pages to the history of this tune. It finds the earliest trace in a book of 1719 with the cheerful title of *D'Urfey's Pills to Purge Melancholy*, where it is set to the words of a ballad called *Gilderoy*. As the *Journal* says, the version in this book is 'so badly barred as to make nonsense', and only the general outline of the tune and a couple of motifs are recognisable as a possible ancestor of Mr Dingle's tune.

Gilderoy was 'a notorious Perthshire freebooter' who was hanged in 1638. The tune is found in several Scottish collections, but the *Journal of the Folk-Song Society* insists it is 'essentially English' (without explaining why). The fact that there are so many variants of the tune, often with only the slightest genetic relationship, seems to suggest it was already an old melody when D'Urfey first published it.

Now let us, finally, return to Kingsfold. One of the variants of *Gilderoy* published by the Folk-Song Society was the tune that Vaughan Williams had heard sung in the Wheatsheaf in 1904, to the words of *The Ballad of Maria Martin*. This is the tune that Mr Booker sang:

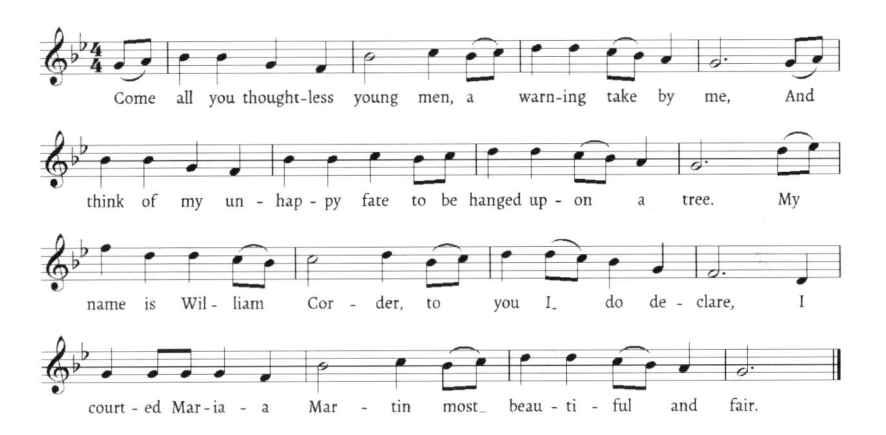

[Musical notation with lyrics:]
Come all you thoughtless young men, a warning take by me, And think of my unhappy fate to be hanged upon a tree. My name is William Corder, to you I do declare, I courted Maria-a Martin most beautiful and fair.

In the *Journal* there are four variants of this tune collected by Vaughan Williams: two from Mr Whitby in Tilney All Saints, Norfolk, one by Mr and Mrs Verrall of Monks Gate, and Mr Booker's version. (We will meet the Verralls again soon when we go to Monks Gate: it is only a few miles from Kingsfold, on the other side of Horsham.) Vaughan Williams comments: 'There seems to be some subtle connection between the words of "Maria Martin" and "Come all you worthy Christians", as they are so often sung to variants of the same tune.'

The Voice from Galilee

The Folk-Song Society published Vaughan Williams' four versions of the 'Maria Martin' tune, labelling two of them Æolian, one Dorian and one Myxolydian, according to which musical mode they were in. And things might have stopped there. The tunes could have stayed in Volume II of the *Journal of the Folk-Song Society* without further troubling anyone but those who delighted in the Æolian and Myxolydian modes. But when Vaughan Williams heard Mr Booker singing in Kingsfold, he had already agreed to be music editor of *The English Hymnal*, and was on the lookout for tunes that could be fitted to the words hymns that Percy Dearmer was sending his way. As well as using tunes that were originally meant to be sung to sacred words, he began to adapt some of the folk-songs that he collected on his travels, and turn them into hymns. In this way he took the tune for *The Ballad of Maria Martin* and fitted it to *I heard the voice of Jesus say*.

The words of this hymn come from a poem called *The Voice from Galilee*, first published in a collection of sacred verse entitled *Hymns of Faith and Hope* (1857), by Horatius Bonar. Bonar was one of the founders of the Free Church of Scotland, formed after the Great Disruption of 1843 in which 450 ministers broke away from the established Church of Scotland. He was a prolific author and poet, supplying many new hymns for the new Church, which hitherto had relied mainly on metrical versions of the Psalms. Here is the first verse of *The Voice from Galilee*:

> *I heard the voice of Jesus say,*
> *Come unto me and rest;*
> *Lay down, thou weary one, lay down*
> *Thy head upon my breast.*
> *I came to Jesus as I was,*
> *Weary, and worn, and sad,*
> *I found in Him a resting-place,*
> *And he has made me glad.*

KINGSFOLD

In *Hymns Ancient & Modern* it had appeared set to the tune VOX DILECTI by J B Dykes:

[Musical notation with lyrics:]

I heard the voice of Je-sus say, 'Come un-to me and rest;
Lay down, thou wear-y one, lay down Thy head up-on my breast:'
I came to Je-sus as I was, Wear-y and worn and sad;
I found in him a rest-ing place, And he has made me glad.

> **John Bacchus Dykes (1823–1876)** was born in Kingston upon Hull, the son of a banker. During his time at St Catherine's College, Cambridge he founded the University Musical Society. Shortly after graduating he was ordained as deacon, and later became precentor at Durham Cathedral.
>
> Dykes wrote nearly 300 hymn-tunes, many of which appeared in *Hymns Ancient & Modern*. Several of his tunes are familiar to this day, and it is still almost unthinkable to have a hymn-book that does not include such standards as MELITA (*Eternal Father, strong to save*), NICAEA (*Holy, holy, holy*) and GERONTIUS (*Praise to the Holiest in the height*). He had a particular fondness for naming his tunes after places—and sometimes people—from the north of England: RIEVAULX is a notable example, named after the abbey in Yorkshire.

Vaughan Williams allowed several of Dykes' tunes into *The English Hymnal*, so he clearly didn't always object to his music. But when it came to *I heard the voice of Jesus say*, he decided not to include Dykes' tune. It is a slightly odd melody, with a strange change from minor to major halfway through, perhaps intending to reflect the structure of the poem, in which each verse has four lines of hearing Jesus's voice followed by four lines of response. Maybe Vaughan Williams was uncomfortable with this mid-stream modulation; maybe he found VOX DILECTI a bit too plodding; or perhaps he just disliked it. Whatever the reason, he decided to find a new tune to fit these words.

I wonder whether the words of Jesus in the poem, 'Come unto me and rest,' reminded Vaughan Williams subconsciously of the opening of the *Maria Martin* ballad, 'Come all you thoughtless young men.' I can't think of any other reason why he would link the two, since Bonar's words have quite a different sentiment from the story of the murder in the Red Barn, or indeed from the dour folk-carol *Come all ye faithful Christians* with which the ballad shares a tune. But he did link them, and the hymn was printed in *The English Hymnal* with the tune KINGSFOLD.

At a public talk I did on the subject of hymn-tunes and place-names I asked the audience which of the two tunes they preferred, KINGSFOLD or VOX DILECTI. The majority voted for KINGSFOLD. But one wise musician who was present qualified this opinion. Perhaps KINGSFOLD is the better tune, he said; but VOX DILECTI is a better tune *for those words*.

Five Variants

But should the tune we know as KINGSFOLD really have been given this title?

The tune that found its way into *The English Hymnal* under this name is slightly different from the version Mr Booker sang to Vaughan Williams in the Wheatsheaf in 1904. Indeed none of the variants of *Gilderoy* published by the Folk-Song Society matches the hymn-tune exactly. The Kingsfold version is the closest, and we might be tempted to think that Vaughan Williams just amended it to make it into a better hymn-tune, as he did with many other folk-song adaptations in *The English Hymnal* and elsewhere. But the truth is that Vaughan Williams used a different variant of the tune, one that had been published in *English County Songs*, a collection edited by Lucy Broadwood and J Alec Fuller Maitland in 1893. In that book the tune is set to the words of a song called *Dives and Lazarus*.

As it happens, these words had been published in the same edition of the *Journal of the Folk-Song Society* as the tune Vaughan Williams collected in Kingsfold; but there they had been set to a completely different melody. In *English County Songs* Lucy Broadwood says that there is no evidence that the words of *Dives and Lazarus* were associated with the *Gilderoy* tune: she just thought they sounded nice together:

> It is not claimed that these words belong to the beautiful tune here given, but they suit it so well that there is a great probability of their having at one time been associated together.

Lucy Broadwood's tune for *Dives and Lazarus* is virtually identical to the tune that Vaughan Williams named KINGSFOLD; indeed it seems she collected royalties for the tune after it was published in *The English Hymnal*. In *English County Songs* the tune is labelled 'Middlesex', so it would seem that Kingsfold in Sussex does not after all deserve all the credit for this hymn-tune.

Many years after his trip to the Wheatsheaf, Vaughan Williams was asked by the British Council to provide some music for the 1939 World's Fair in New York. As he so often did, he turned to folk-song for inspiration and produced a work for harp and strings based on different versions of the 'Maria Martin' tune. With Lucy Broadwood's version in mind, he called the work *Five Variants of Dives and Lazarus*.

❖

OUR NEXT TUNE is another folk-song adaptation by Vaughan Williams, one with deep connections to a book that obsessed him for most of his adult life. The place after which the tune is named is not far from Kingsfold.

Chapter 11
MONKS GATE

Monks Gate

He who would valiant be

He who would val-iant be 'Gainst all dis-as-ter,

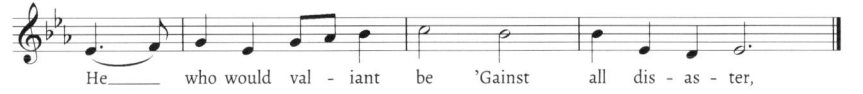

ENGLISH FOLKSONG, ADAPTED BY RALPH VAUGHAN WILLIAMS 1872-1958[1]

MONKS GATE IS A HAMLET to the south-east of Horsham in West Sussex. The name is first recorded in the seventeenth century; the 'Monk' bit seems to be a family name, and the 'Gate' refers to an entrance into St Leonard's Forest.

This forest to the east of Horsham is notable for being the place where the last known dragon in England lived. In the 6th century, the eponymous St Leonard fought a dragon in the forest. It wounded him, and where his blood fell, white lilies immediately sprang up. He beat it in the end, though, and for his prize he prayed that snakes would be banished from the forest, and that nightingales would sing no more there (because they had interrupted him in his prayers).

I don't know if nightingales sing there now, but Leonard did not succeed in getting rid of the dragons. In 1614 a pamphlet was published, containing:

> A True and Wonderfull Discourse relating a strange and monstrous Serpent (or Dragon) lately discovered, and yet living, to the great Annoyance and divers Slaughters both of Men and Cattell, by his strong and violent Poyson. In Sussex, two miles from Horsam, in a Woode called St Leonards Forrest, and thirtie miles from London, this present month of August, 1614.

---

[1] MONKS GATE English traditional melody collected, adapted & arranged by Ralph Vaughan Williams (1872-1958) from *The English Hymnal*. Extract reproduced by permission of Oxford University Press. All rights reserved.

O LITTLE TOWN

The pamphlet must be true as well as wonderful, because it mentions four specific people who had seen the dragon: John Steele, Christopher Holder, and a 'Widow Woman dwelling near Faygate', as well as the carrier of Horsham 'who lieth at the White Horse in Southwarke.' (I think even in 1614 the word 'lie' had more than one meaning, but the tales one heard in pubs were just as true as they are today.)

Thrift Cottages, Monks Gate.
This is the street, if not the actual house, where Peter and Harriet Verrall lived.

Songs by the fireside

Monks Gate can claim to be the source for not one but three of the best-known hymn-tunes in the repertoire, all of which we owe to one couple. In the early years of the twentieth century the hamlet was home to Peter and Harriet Verrall, who lived in Thrift Cottages in Nuthurst Road. Harriet had been born in nearby Slaugham, and Peter—a farm labourer—was originally from Lewes.

The Verralls possessed a great store of folk-songs. In 1905 the *West Sussex Gazette* ran a competition for the best traditional Sussex tune, and Harriet Verrall won first prize for versions of two folk-songs, *Covent Garden* and *Salisbury Plain*. The judge in this competition was Lucy Broadwood, who was secretary of the Folk-Song Society.

> **Lucy Broadwood (1858–1929)** was the great-granddaughter of John Broadwood (1732–1812), founder of the eminent piano manufacturing company whose customers included Ludwig van Beethoven. A gifted pianist and singer, Lucy grew up in Lyne House in Surrey, where as a girl she first encountered folk-culture when the mummers came visiting at Christmas. She later became a keen collector of folksongs, and in 1893 she published *English Country Songs* together with John Alexander Fuller Maitland.
>
> She was one of the founding members of the Folk-Song Society in 1898, becoming its Honorary Secretary in 1904. She became President of the Society in 1928 following the death of Lord Tennyson (son of the great poet).

The previous year Harriet had sung both these songs to Ralph Vaughan Williams, who published them in the *Journal of the Folk-Song Society*. In his *West Sussex Village Book* (1984), Tony Wales recounts a visit in about 1959 to their son Frederick Verrall, who recalled his parents singing to each other by the fire in the evenings. Frederick also remembered Vaughan Williams and 'another man' visiting his parents on more than one occasion and listening to their songs. Sometimes they would record them on a phonograph.

Sussex tunes

Among the archives of the English Folk Dance and Song Society (the successor to Cecil Sharp's Folk-Song Society) is a manuscript showing two versions of a song about a shipwreck, called *The Royal George*. The first variant is noted as having been collected by 'RVW & GSKB' from a

O Little Town

Mr Robert Hurn of Southwold in Suffolk. The second was noted by GSKB in 1911, sung by Mr Verrall.

RVW is, of course, Ralph Vaughan Williams. GSKB was George Sainton Kaye Butterworth. I would guess that Butterworth was the 'other man' whom Frederick Verrall remembered accompanying Vaughan Williams on his visits to Monks Gate.

> **George Butterworth (1885–1916)** was born in London and educated at Eton and Trinity College Oxford, where he studied Greats (Classics). While at Oxford he pursued his interest in music and became the President of the university music club.
>
> After a brief spell teaching at Radley College he enrolled at the Royal College of Music, where his teachers included Charles Wood. Butterworth's interest in traditional arts began while he was at university. He became an enthusiastic collector of folksongs and folkdances. He was a leading figure in both the Folk-Song Society and its sister project, the Folk Dance Society; indeed if anything he was more interested in dance than music, and was an accomplished morris man.
>
> His friendship with Vaughan Williams also dates from his time at Oxford. Vaughan Williams' *London Symphony* was dedicated to Butterworth, who left most of his manuscripts to RVW. His output as a composer is relatively small—owing to his tragically short life—but it is highly accomplished. He is best known for his settings of the poetry of A E Houseman, *A Shropshire Lad*, as well as the orchestral *Rhapsody* developoed from those songs, and other miniatures like *The Banks of Green Willow*, based on folksongs from Sussex.
>
> At the outbreak of war in August 1914 Butterworth enlisted in the Army. In the summer of 1916 he was twice awarded the Military Cross. The second time was for his bravery on 5th August; on that day, at the first battle of the Somme, he was killed by an enemy bullet to the head.

Here is the version of *The Royal George* that Peter Verrall sang to Butterworth (I have had to change the rhythm slightly from the manuscript, to make the notes fit the words):

As we set sail for the rock of Gibraltar, As we set sail from sweet Dublin Bay, O little did we think of our sad misfortune, Sleeping in the briny sea.

A variant of this tune was adapted by Vaughan Williams to fit the words of *Father, hear the prayer we offer*. In *The English Hymnal* and subsequent hymn-books the tune is known simply as SUSSEX.

The second hymn-tune contributed by the Verralls was another one that Harriet submitted to the *West Sussex Gazette* for their competition. It did not win, but it has since become very well known indeed. The words are *On Christmas Night all Christians sing*, and the tune has become known as the SUSSEX CAROL. It was first published by Vaughan Williams in *Eight Traditional English Carols* (1919).

The third tune that Vaughan Williams took from the Verralls was the one he named MONKS GATE. This is the tune that Harriet sang to him, as published in the *Journal of the Folk-Song Society*:

Our Captain calls all hands on board tomorrow Leaving my dear to mourn in grief and sorrow. Dry up those briny tears and leave off weeping, So happy we may be at our next meeting.

O Little Town

There are a number of different variations of the words as well as the music. A common version runs as follows:

Our captain cried all hands and away tomorrow,
Leaving these girls behind in grief and sorrow.
What makes you go abroad, fighting for strangers
When you could stop at home, free from all dangers?

The melody is also sung to a song called *A blacksmith courted me*:

For a blacksmith courted me, nine months or better.
And he who gained my heart wrote me a letter.
With his hammer in his hand strikes his blows so clever
And if I was with my love, I'd live forever.

The tune has an ABBC structure. That is to say, it is made up of four phrases, the second and third of which are the same: so the notes for 'Leaving my dear to mourn in grief and sorrow' are the same as the notes for 'Dry up those briny tears and leave off weeping.' The first and last phrases, while not identical, share certain patterns: the notes for 'at our next meeting' seem to echo '...hands on board tomorrow.' What is perhaps strange, though, is that the pattern of the musical phrases is at odds with the way the song rhymes, which is AABB: the first and second lines have one rhyme (tomorrow/sorrow), and the third and fourth have another (weeping/meeting).

I'm doing all this structural analysis because it is relevant to the way Vaughan Williams adapted the tune when he came to use it for a hymn. The tune that we know as MONKS GATE has an AABC structure, so it is the first phrase of music that gets repeated, not the second. In this form it has become so familiar that when you hear the original folk-song version of the tune it can take you by surprise.

The slow growth of an opera

The words to which Vaughan Williams fitted this tune came from one of his favourite books, *The Pilgrim's Progress*. He was captivated by Bunyan's allegory of a traveller trying to make his way to the Celestial City. He had first come across the story when he was a boy, and in 1906 he was asked to provide some incidental music for a theatrical version being staged at Reigate Priory. Into this music he wove a hymn-tune—not MONKS GATE but the one called YORK. The melody for this tune came from a *Scottish Psalter* of 1615, but the harmony (first printed in Ravenscroft's *The Whole Booke of Psalmes*) was by the composer John Milton, father of the author of *Paradise Lost*. It therefore comes trailing clouds of Roundhead glory and is a fitting backdrop for a tale by Bunyan, who—like Milton—was a supporter of the Parliamentarian cause during the Civil War.

Vaughan Williams was 34 in 1906. The incidental music for *The Pilgrim's Progress* sparked an interest in the book which lasted the rest of his life. The idea of turning Bunyan's story into an opera was one that he returned to over and over again throughout many decades. At different times he set to music various scenes and extracts from the book, including an extended scene called *The Shepherds of the Delectable Mountains*, parts of which date back to the Reigate Priory production.

Fearing the opera might never be finished, Vaughan Williams re-used much of the music in his magnificent Fifth Symphony, which was first performed in 1943. Finally, in 1951, when he was in his late 70s, the complete opera was staged. It begins and ends with the hymn-tune YORK, which had featured in that Reigate event nearly half a century earlier.

The opera—or 'Morality' as Vaughan Williams came to call it—is rarely staged today. English National Opera did a splendid production in 2012, but it is a difficult work to put on, calling for a host of soloists and elaborate staging. Many years ago I sang in the chorus for a concert version conducted by Leslie Olive in Dorking Halls, near Vaughan Williams' home in Leith Hill. The title role of the Pilgrim was taken by John Noble, who had sung the part in the 1950s while at Cambridge, in one of the earliest productions of the piece. (In Bunyan's book, by the way, the protagonist is called Christian; but Vaughan Williams wanted his morality to be more universal, and renamed the character simply Pilgrim.)

Among the scenes which Vaughan Williams included in his opera is a song that comes from Part 2 of *The Pilgrim's Progress*, which charts the journey of Christian's wife, Christiana, and their children. These are the words as Bunyan wrote them:

> *Who would true valour see,*
> *Let him come hither;*
> *One here will constant be,*
> *Come wind, come weather*
> *There's no discouragement*
> *Shall make him once relent*
> *His first avow'd intent*
> *To be a pilgrim.*
>
> *Whoso beset him round*
> *With dismal stories,*
> *Do but themselves confound;*
> *His strength the more is.*
> *No lion can him fright,*
> *He'll with a giant fight,*
> *But he will have a right*
> *To be a pilgrim.*
>
> *Hobgoblin nor foul fiend*
> *Can daunt his spirit;*
> *He knows he at the end*
> *Shall life inherit.*

MONKS GATE

Then fancies fly away,
He'll not fear what men say;
He'll labour night and day
To be a pilgrim.

In the book these words are sung by a character called Mr Valiant-for-Truth, 'a man with his Sword drawn, and his Face all bloody'. Vaughan Williams set them unchanged in his opera, giving them a new and vigorous tune:[2]

This tune is quite different from the one that is associated with these words in the hymn-books. Occasionally you will read that the opera includes the hymn-tune, but this is not true. I don't know if the tune from the opera has ever been used in a church context; it might make an interesting alternative to the usual tune, and has the advantage that it forces singers to put the stress on the first syllable of 'pilgrim', avoiding the awkward 'pil-GRIM' that so often happens.

Down with hobgoblins!

Who would true valour see was first used as a hymn in 1873 in a book brought out by E Paxton Hood, a minister from Brighton. The book was called simply *Our Hymn Book*; it was a collection made especially for use in his church, and did not have a wide circulation.

---

[2] *The Pilgrim's Progress (A Morality)* by Ralph Vaughan Williams, founded on John Bunyan's allegory of the same name. © Oxford University Press 1952. Libretto adapted by the composer from Bunyan, with interpolations from the Bible, and verses by Ursula Wood. Extract reproduced by permission. All rights reserved.

The song had also caught the eye of Percy Dearmer, the editor of *The English Hymnal*. He thought the imagery of pilgrimage would be appropriate for a hymn. However, he took issue with some of Bunyan's words; or rather, he was afraid that his congregation would. He therefore took the liberty of re-writing parts of the lyric to make it more suitable.

The first thing Dearmer did was to make the words more personal. Bunyan's lines speak about a third-person pilgrim: let *him* come hither. Dearmer kept this focus for the first two verses of his hymn, but in the last one he allowed his congregation to apply the words to themselves, so '*He* knows *he* at the end...' becomes '*We* know *we* at the end...'

Secondly, Dearmer did away with the hobgoblin. Many people have lamented this cruel expulsion—after all, what has the poor goblin ever done to us? But we have to remember that this was not then an established hymn, and it may never have become one if Dearmer had not removed words which might have caused sniggering among the congregation. Only now, when the hymn has become part of the shared heritage of church music, can editors decide to restore Bunyan's original.

Here are the words as they were published in *The English Hymnal*. I have underlined Dearmer's amendments:

<u>He who would valiant be</u>
<u>'Gainst all disaster,</u>
<u>Let him in constancy</u>
<u>Follow the Master.</u>
There's no discouragement
Shall make him once relent
His first avowed intent
To be a pilgrim.

Who so beset him round
With dismal stories,
Do but themselves confound—
His strength the more is.

<u>No foes shall stay his might,</u>
<u>Though he with giants fight:</u>
<u>He will make good his</u> right
To be a pilgrim.

<u>Since, Lord, thou dost defend</u>
<u>Us with thy Spirit,</u>
<u>We know we</u> at the end
Shall life inherit.
Then fancies <u>flee</u> away!
<u>I'll fear not</u> what men say,
<u>I'll</u> labour night and day
To be a pilgrim.

The tune that Vaughan Williams used for Dearmer's hymn was a variation on *Our Captain Calls*. He made the rhythm more regular, and repeated the first phrase of music instead of the second. It is in this form that the tune has become familiar as MONKS GATE, and sung with gusto up and down the land. Among the schools which have adopted it as their school song is Reigate Grammar, close to the place where Vaughan Williams first thought of putting Bunyan to music.

A question of punctuation

When the tune was printed in *The English Hymnal* it was called MONKS GATE. In some more recent publications, including current editions of *Hymns Ancient & Modern*, it is called MONK'S GATE, with an apostrophe. This might seem to be more correct; but the locals think otherwise. All the road-signs in the area refer to the hamlet as Monks Gate, with no apostrophe; and the elaborate and elegant sign erected in 2000 also proudly does away with all punctuation. So MONKS GATE it is.

Millennium sign, Monks Gate.

❖

OUR NEXT AND FINAL DESTINATION is *O little town* itself.

Chapter 12
FOREST GREEN

FOREST GREEN

O little town of Bethlehem

O lit - tle town of Beth - le - hem, How still we see thee lie!

MELODY FROM AN ENGLISH FOLKSONG

O *LITTLE TOWN OF BETHLEHEM* is one of the rock-solid favourites without which no Christmas would be complete. Unlike many hymns and carols that refer to places named in the Bible, its description of the 'little town' of the Nativity came from direct personal experience. Its author was the Bostonian cleric Phillips Brooks (1835-1893), who is remembered in America as one of the outstanding preachers of the 19th century. In 1865 he visited Bethlehem and saw for himself some of the places associated with the Christmas story:

> Before dark, we rode out of town to the field where they say the shepherds saw the star... as we passed, the shepherds were still 'keeping watch over their flocks', or leading them home to fold.

Back home at his church in Philadelphia, he wrote the now-familiar words for his Sunday school to sing, recalling how he had witnessed first-hand the silent stars shining above the deep and dreamless sleep of Bethlehem. The new carol was scheduled to be sung at a service one Sunday in 1868. Brooks had asked the organist at Holy Trinity Church, Lewis Redner, to write a tune for it; but inspiration failed him all the way up to the night before the service. That night, Redner was woken from his sleep by 'an angel strain whispering in my ear', supposedly dictating the tune to him. (This is not the only example of music coming to the composer in a dream: Paul McCartney famously composed *Yesterday* in his sleep, and both Stravinsky and Schumann had dreams in which they heard music that they remembered and wrote down when they awoke.)

O little town of Bethlehem was printed in leaflet form by Richard McCauley, a bookshop owner in Philadelphia; and later it was included in *The Church Porch*, a collection of hymns published in 1874, together with Redner's tune, which was given the name ST LOUIS. This name seems to have been chosen by the book's publisher, William R Huntingdon, perhaps in a punning reference to the composer's first name. St Louis is over 800 miles from Philadelphia, so as far as I know there is no other obvious reason for picking that name.

These days only four verses of the carol are usually sung, but in the original there were five. The missing fourth verse goes as follows:

> *Where children pure and happy*
>   *Pray to the Blessèd Child,*
> *Where misery cries out to thee,*
>   *Son of the mother mild;*
> *Where charity stands watching*
>   *And faith holds wide the door,*
> *The dark night wakes, the glory breaks,*
>   *And Christmas comes once more.*

In the USA the carol is still inseparably associated with the tune ST LOUIS. In Britain, where Brooks' words were first published in 1896, it is sometimes heard sung to a tune by Walford Davies called simply CHRISTMAS CAROL, and rarely to another one by the same composer, called WENGEN (a village in Switzerland). But most British carol-singers would probably consider the 'proper' tune to be the one first published in *The English Hymnal* in 1906.

Forest Green

There is more than one place called Forest Green. Nailsworth in Gloucestershire is home to Forest Green Rovers, a proud football club who proclaim themselves to be 'the longest serving member of the Football Conference', which is the tier of the footballing hierarchy below the Football League. The club takes its name from an actual green half a mile from Nailsworth; but it has absolutely nothing to do with hymns. There is a street in Bracknell called Forest Green, and one in Holyport in Berkshire; neither of these are connected with hymn-tunes, either. Forest Green is also a colour, supposed to represent the colour of leaves.

The Forest Green after which our hymn-tune is named is in Surrey. It cannot in all conscience call itself a town, even a little one. Its own website describes it as 'a hamlet whose origin is vague'. In the past it has been known as Folles Green, Farleys Green and Ferles Green, suggesting that perhaps the more picturesque Forest Green is a later corruption of a name that maybe had nothing to do with woodlands.

The village, or hamlet, lies roughly at the centre of a circle whose circumference passes through Dorking, Crawley, Horsham and Guildford. Maps from around the end of the nineteenth century show it as a loose collection of buildings rather than a village: there is a Forest Green Mill (complete with a millpond), a Forest Green House, a smithy and a pub—the Parrot—which dates back 400 years and is thriving to this day. The church, Holy Trinity, is nowhere near as old: it was built in 1896 in memory of Everard Hensley, a young man who was killed in a shooting accident in 1892. Before then there was no church in Forest Green.

The Ploughboy's Dream

In December 1903 Vaughan Williams was at Broadmoor—not the secure psychiatric hospital in Berkshire, but a small gathering of buildings in Surrey, about a mile north of his home in Leith Hill. As with his visits to Kingsfold and Monks Gate, he was there on a mission to collect folk-songs. I believe this particular collecting expedition occurred at the house of Frederick Longhurst, who was aged 43 at the time. Two of the songs Vaughan Williams heard at Broadmoor were sung to him by Isaac

O Little Town

Longhurst, a resident of Forest Green who was born in 1833. Frederick was not Isaac's son, but it seems likely that they were related, and I am willing to guess that it was in Frederick's house that Vaughan Williams heard Isaac sing his songs.

The tune we know as FOREST GREEN was not sung by Isaac Longhurst, but by a Mr Garman. It is generally called *The Ploughboy's Dream*, though it is more like a nightmare. This is the song as Vaughan Williams heard it:

> *I am a ploughboy stout and strong as ever drove a team.*
> *Now three years since I slept in bed I had an awful dream:*
> *Now since the dream has done me good, I'll put it down in rhyme,*
> *That other boys might read and sing, whenever they have time.*
>
> *I dreamt I drove my master's team with Dobbin, Bald and Star,*
> *Before a stiff and handy plough, as all my master's are.*
> *I found the ground was baked so hard, 'twas more like bricks than clay,*
> *I could not cut my furrow through, nor would my beasts obey.*
>
> *Now Dobbin lay down, both Bald and Star they kicked and snorted sore,*
> *The more I lashed and cursed and swore the less my cattle stir.*
> *Then lo, above me a bright youth did seem to hang in air.*
> *With purple wings and golden hands, as angels painted are.*

Vaughan Williams then notes 'Mr Garman only remembered fragments of the words.' The rest of the song, which Mr Garman had apparently forgotten, goes as follows:

> *'Give over, cruel wretch,' he cried, 'nor thus thy beasts abuse.*
> *Think, if the ground was not as hard, would they their work refuse?*
> *Besides, I heard thee curse and swear, as if dumb beasts could know,*
> *What all thy oaths and curses meant, or better for them go.*
>
> *But though they know not, there is one who knows thy sins full well,*

And what shall be thine after doom another shall thee tell.'
No more he said, but, light as air, he vanished from my sight;
And with him went the sun's bright beams, and all was dark as night.

The thunder roared from underground, the earth did seem to gape;
Blue flames broke forth, and in those flames, a dire, gigantic shape.
'Soon shall I call thee mine,' it cried, with voice so drear and deep,
That, quivering like an aspen leaf, I wakened from my sleep.

Vaughan Williams noted that Mr Garman, 'though living now in Surrey, is a native of Sussex', and estimated his age at 'about 60'. The singer was Henry Garman, who was born in Horsham in 1830, so he would actually have been 73 at the time he sang *The Ploughboy's Dream* at Broadmoor in 1903. He told Vaughan Williams that he used to sing this song to the Revd John Broadwood, an early collector of folksongs (and uncle of Lucy Broadwood). For this, Broadwood paid him half-a-crown per rendition; we do not know if Vaughan Williams took the hint and paid up.

The nightmare becomes a carol

The English Hymnal of 1906 published *O little town of Bethlehem* complete with the now-rare fourth verse quoted above. It also changed the second verse, which in Phillips Brooks' original began 'For Christ is born of Mary...' and only in the second half of the verse brought in the lines 'O morning stars together...' Presumably it was Percy Dearmer who decided to switch the two halves of the verse round, which seems to make much more sense.

The tune to which it is set is a fairly faithful version of *The Ploughboy's Dream*. As usual, Vaughan Williams made a few changes to the melody to make it more suitable for singing as a hymn: most notably, lengthening the first note of the penultimate line. It has become a staple of British carol services. The beautiful words with their images of quiet and peace seem to go well with the simple and memorable tune, and they have become so closely associated that it is a bit of a shock to hear the original folksong, with its terrible vision of hell.

Why Forest Green?

In the Journal of the Folk-Song Society *The Ploughboy's Dream* is described as having been sung at Forest Green in December 1903. In fact, as we have seen, Vaughan Williams heard it at Broadmoor, a good three miles away from Forest Green. So how did the tune acquire this name? You will often read that Mr Garman was a resident of Forest Green; but the 1901 census shows he was living at Stane Street, Ockley. This is not far from Forest Green, but not close enough to be considered actually in the village. Earlier censuses show that he spent much of his life in Sheep Green (sometimes spelt Ship Green), an area to the north of Jayes Park, halfway between Leith Hill and Ockley. Again, this is in the vicinity, but it is definitely not Forest Green itself. Either Henry Garman had moved between 1901 and 1903, or Vaughan Williams made a mistake (perhaps confusing the notes he made about Garman with those that referred to Isaac Longhurst). It must be admitted that FOREST GREEN is a simple, poetic name for a beautiful tune; though in some ways perhaps SHEEP GREEN would have been more appropriate, remembering Phillips Brooks' visit to Bethlehem and the fields where the angel supposedly proclaimed the Nativity to the terrified shepherds who were abiding there.

❖

OUR JOURNEY IS ALMOST ENDED. Our search for places that are associated with hymn-tunes has taken us all over Britain from Scotland to Sussex, from the mountains of Wales to the flatlands of East Anglia, and occasionally overseas. But I have only really scratched the surface. Place-names have been used as a source for the names of hymn-tunes for hundreds of years, and there are many more 'little towns' to see. So before I close, let's have one more flick through the hymn-book and take a look at some of the places we haven't visited in this book.

Chapter 13

EVERYWHERE ELSE

Everywhere else

Earth hath many a noble city

There are many reasons for naming a hymn-tune after a place. In the early days of Este and Ravenscroft it was just a simple way of identifying the tune, referring to a church or cathedral, college or school where the tune was commonly sung, or to the place from which it originated. Once this practice was established, it became common to give tunes the name of the place where they were composed, or of a place that was important to the composer.

In this book I have touched on just a dozen or so tunes. The ones I have chosen are reasonably well-known and—in *most* cases—they are tunes I like. There is also a story to tell about how they got their name. But there are many other 'little towns' whose story I have not had time to tell.

For instance, we could have spent a lot more time in Wales, where a host of places have lent their names to hymn-tunes. There is Aberystwyth by Joseph Parry (1841–1903), one of the earliest Welsh tunes to have been accepted in English hymn-books; it is usually sung to *Jesu, lover of my soul*. Or we might have travelled to Blaenwern, a farm in Pembrokeshire, where a young boy called Tom, the son of composer William Penfro Rowlands (1860–1937), recovered from childhood pneumonia; his father immortalised the place in the wonderful tune commonly sung to *Love divine, all loves excelling*. Another sturdy Welsh tune is the one called Llanfair, by Robert Williams (1781–1821) which was used in *The English Hymnal* for the Ascension hymn *Hail the day that sees him rise*; thankfully for the editors of hymn-books, in Williams' day the little town in Anglesey from which it takes its title had not yet acquired its modern name, Llanfairpwllgwyngyllgogerychwyrndrobwllllantysiliogogogoch.

While we were on the western shores of Britain, it would have been just a short sea-crossing to Ireland, where we could have taken a look at SLANE, a village in County Meath from which we have the tune for *Lord of all hopefulness*.

Back in England, we could have gone to CRANHAM in Gloucestershire, where Gustav Holst's mother used to play the harmonium in church; his famous tune for *In the bleak midwinter* was probably composed there, in a house that has since been renamed Midwinter Cottage. A trip to Oxford could have taken in WOLVERCOTE, a grand tune for *O Jesus I have promised* by William Ferguson (1874–1950); and while we were there we could also have seen BLACKBIRD LEYS (composed by Peter Cutts, b.1937) and SUMMERTOWN (my own tune for *Christ is our corner-stone*). A visit to Cambridge would give us a chance to see COE FEN, a meadow near the Leys School, where the composer of the wonderful tune for *How shall I sing that majesty*, Kenneth Naylor (1931–1991), was music master. Still in East Anglia, we might have gone to SAFFRON WALDEN, a town that a Spaniard once described to me as the most boring place on earth, but which has nevertheless given us A H Brown's lovely tune for *Just as I am*. Then we could have driven up a very narrow lane in search of LITTLE CORNARD, where the composer Martin Shaw (1875–1958) spent his honeymoon, and after which he named his rousing tune that is sung to *Hills of the north, rejoice*.

We had a quick look at YORK when we were passing through Monks Gate; and there is also a tune that occasionally takes the name of YORKSHIRE, sung to the words of the Christmas hymn *Christians awake, salute the happy dawn*. This tune also answers to the name of STOCKPORT, which of course is not in Yorkshire, but in Greater Manchester, and thus belongs to the old rival, Lancashire. The composer of the tune was John Wainwright (1723–1768); his family had connections with Stockport, and it is sometimes said that he was organist at the parish church there. Yorkshire's claims to the tune are quite groundless.

The 'national anthem' of Yorkshire, *On Ilkla Moor baht 'at*, is also an immigrant to God's own county. It was composed by Thomas Clark (1775–1859), a Wesleyan boot-maker's son from Canterbury. As a hymn-tune it is called CRANBROOK, after a village in Kent, and was originally used for *Grace, 'tis a charming sound* by Philip Doddridge (1702–1751). These days you will occasionally hear it sung to the words of *While shepherds watched their flocks by night*.

HELMSLEY is, however, definitely in Yorkshire. This tune, sung to the words of the great Advent hymn *Lo! he comes with clouds descending*, is now thought of as one of the great splendid jewels of hymnody. But its origins are much more lowly. It probably started life as an aria in a satirical comic opera called *The Golden Pippin*, by Kane O'Hara (1711–1782), which was nearly banned by the Lord Chamberlain for being rude about the royal family. The tune was adapted by Thomas Olivers (1725–1799), an associate of John Wesley, and then adopted by Richard Conyers (1725–1786), an evangelical clergyman from Yorkshire, who gave it the name HELMSLEY after the parish where he was rector from 1756.

The ancient capital of England, Winchester, has given us two tunes: WINCHESTER OLD (*While shepherds watched their flocks by night*) and WINCHESTER NEW (*On Jordan's bank the Baptist's cry*). And the present-day capital could practically furnish a hymn-book by itself, for the map of London is simply bristling with the names of hymn-tunes. LONDON is a tune by J Sheeles (1688–1761) for Joseph Addison's poem *The spacious firmament on high*; while LONDON NEW is a melody for *God moves in a mysterious way*; evidently the tune's movements are equally baffling, for it started life a long way from London, in *The Scottish Psalter*. WESTMINSTER is the tune for *My God, how wonderful thou art*, by James Turle (1802–1882), while WESTMINSTER ABBEY—sung to *Christ is made the sure foundation*—is a tune as grand and solid as the Abbey itself, composed by Henry Purcell (1659–1695). ST GEORGE'S WINDSOR, by George Elvey (1816–1893) is the Harvest hymn *Come, ye thankful people, come*; REGENT SQUARE, by Henry Smart (1818–1879) is *Light's abode, celestial Salem*; DUKE STREET, by John Hatton

O LITTLE TOWN

(d. 1793) is *Fight the good fight*. ENGLANDS LANE, named after a street in NW3 near Belsize Park, is *For the beauty of the earth*, composed by Geoffrey Shaw (1879–1943), the brother of Martin Shaw. There are tunes called HAMMERSMITH by both William Charles Filby (1833–1913) and William Henry Gladstone (1840–1892). RICHMOND is one of the tunes used for *Praise to the Holiest in the height*; the tune is by Thomas Haweis (1731–1820) and the harmony by Samuel Webbe the younger (1770–1843), who gave it its name, not in honour of Richmond upon Thames, nor even Richmond in Yorkshire, but for his friend the Revd Leigh Richmond.

We have already been to KINGSFOLD, MONKS GATE and FOREST GREEN; and the hymn-tunes based on folk-songs collected by Vaughan Williams, Cecil Sharp, Lucy Broadwood and their colleagues would provide many more happy weeks of tramping round the British countryside: STALHAM, FARNHAM and HORSHAM; RODMELL and RUSPER; SHEPTON-BEAUCHAMP and SHIPSTON; KING'S LYNN and KING'S LANGLEY (not to mention KING'S WESTON, which is an original tune by RVW, not a folksong).

Nor do we have to confine ourselves to our own shores. MELITA, J B Dykes' tune for *Eternal Father, strong to save*, is the old Latin name for Malta, commemorating a Biblical account of 'those in peril on the sea': St Paul was shipwrecked there. There is a tune called NICAEA, also by Dykes (for *Holy, holy, holy, Lord God Almighty*), named after the ancient city in Turkey which played a key role in the early church and from which we get the Nicene Creed. Still in the Middle East, we know about JERUSALEM, but there is also ANTIOCH (*Joy to the world*, based on a tune by G F Handel) and PETRA (*Rock of ages, cleft for me*, the tune by Richard Redhead, 1820–1901; *petra* is, of course, Latin for 'rock'). In Europe we find SALZBURG, TYROL and VIENNA (as well as INNSBRUCK); BONN, HANOVER, MANNHEIM, NÜRNBERG and STUTTGART; AGINCOURT, BESANÇON, LOURDES and PICARDY; MOSCOW and ST PETERSBURG; and VENICE. Some tunes are named after whole countries: AUSTRIA, of course, but also FINLANDIA, based on the patriotic symphonic poem by Jean Sibelius (1865–1957) and sung to *Be still, my soul: the Lord is on your side*.

And so we could go on. Just about every page of the atlas has a corresponding page in the hymn-book: HEREFORD and GLOUCESTER; BATH and WELLS; LIVERPOOL and EVERTON; ABERDEEN, DUNDEE, DUNFERMLINE and KILMARNOCK; CARLISLE and WINDERMERE; NORTHAMPTON and SOUTHAMPTON; CORNWALL, WILTSHIRE and DEVONSHIRE; SURREY and KENT; SUSSEX, ESSEX and WESSEX. The tradition of associating hymn-tunes with particular localities, whether little towns, noble cities or entire nations, has been deeply ingrained for hundreds of years. Vaughan Williams thought that music was rooted in the soil: it seems that composers of hymn-tunes and editors of hymn-books would agree with him.

Acknowledgements

My thanks are due to the following people, whose help has been invaluable in the preparation of this book:

Robert Canham of The Hymn Society of Great Britain and Ireland, for kindly sending reprints of articles that appeared in the Hymn Society's Journal: particularly those on Abbot's Leigh and Crimond.

Simon Coombs, Chairman of the Vaughan Williams Society, especially for his help in looking into the history of Forest Green.

Marlene Cowie, Church Officer at Crimond, who very kindly opened the church for me, showed me round, and gave me coffee and biscuits.

Nicky Davies of *Church Music Quarterly*, for agreeing to publish an article on *O Little Town* in the December 2014 edition of *CMQ*.

Rachel Ellis, for the loan of several books about Percy Dearmer, Vaughan Williams and *The English Hymnal*.

Jim Farthing, Production Coordinator for BBC Radio Comedy, for help with obtaining permission to use the quotation on page 4; and **Iain Pattinson** and **Colin Sell** for granting that permission.

Michael Haslam and Peter Wright, for reviewing drafts of the book, spotting mistakes and making helpful suggestions.

Menna James of Aberdare Library, for permission to use the picture of Capel Rhondda Welsh Baptist Chapel in Hopkinstown, Pontypridd.

Jenny and David Hansell, John Sherlock, Jo Browse and Hugh Crook, for providing live musical illustrations at the talks I gave on the subject of *O Little Town* in Warnham and Rudgwick.

David Hughes of the Royal Yacht Squadron, for information about Hubert Parry's membership of the Squadron and his gifts to it.

O Little Town

Bruce Munro, for sending me Imogen Holst's article *Gustav Holst and Thaxted*, and other information concerning Holst's connections with Thaxted.

Valerie Ruddle, who started investigating the places that inspired hymn-tunes many years before I did, and kindly sent me her series of booklets on the subject, entitled *Journeys with Tunes*.

… and Jo Browse again, for encouragement, love, and everything else.

Picture credits

Unless otherwise stated, the portraits of people in this book are, to the best of my knowledge, in the public domain. The sources of other pictures and images that I have used are as follows:

Maps

Maps at the beginning of each chapter: © D-Maps.com. Sources are as follows:

England: http://d-maps.com/m/europa/uk/angleterre/angleterre90.gif
Eastern England: http://d-maps.com/m/europa/uk/englandeast/englandeast32.gif
South-west England: http://d-maps.com/m/europa/uk/englandsw/englandsw32.gif
South-east England: http://d-maps.com/m/europa/uk/englandse/englandse32.gif
Wales: http://d-maps.com/m/europa/uk/galles/galles72.gif
Scotland: http://d-maps.com/m/europa/uk/ecosse/ecosse72.gif
Austria: http://d-maps.com/m/europa/austria/autriche/autriche05.gif
Eastern Med: http://d-maps.com/m/mediterranean/meditorient/meditorient28.gif
Europe: http://d-maps.com/m/europa/europemax/europemax18.gif

(The black blobs on these maps, showing the approximate location of the 'little towns' in question, are my own work. Not to be used for navigation.)

Other images

The following photographs are by the author, copyright © Mark Browse: Crimond church clock (p.21); Crimond church (p. 25); Innsbruck decorations (p.31); Holst's house in Thaxted (p.67); Thaxted Church (p.71); Cyril Taylor memorial in Salisbury (p.80); The Old Vicarage, Down Ampney (p.99); The Owl at

O Little Town

Kingsfold (p.108); Thrift Cottages, Monks Gate (p.124); Monks Gate millennium village sign (p.134).

The picture of Capel Rhondda Welsh Baptist Chapel in Hopkinstown, Pontypridd (p90) is used by kind permission of Rhondda Cynon Taff Libraries.

The colour used for the back cover and spine of this book is, of course, Forest Green.

Works Consulted

Hymn books

The following are the hymn-books I have consulted most often, either because of their historical importance or because they happened to be on my shelves:

The Whole Booke of Psalmes, collected into Englishe metre by T. Sternhold, W. Whitingham, I. Hopkins, and others. London: John Day, 1584. (*Sternhold & Hopkins*, otherwise known as *Day's Psalter* or 'The Old Version'.)

The Whole Booke of Psalmes. London: printed by Thomas Este for the Company of Stationers, 1604. (*Este's Psalter*.)

The Whole Booke of Psalmes with the Hymnes Evangelicall, and Songs Spiritual, Newly Corrected and enlarged by Tho: Ravenscroft Bachelor of Musicke. Printed at London for the Company of Stationers, 1621. (*Ravenscroft's Psalter*.)

Hymns Ancient & Modern, for use in the services of the Church. London: Novello, 1861.

The Yattendon Hymnal. London: Oxford University Press, 1899.

The English Hymnal. London: Oxford University Press, 1906; new edition 1933.

Repton School Hymns. London: Oxford University Press, 1924.

Songs of Praise. London: Oxford University Press, 1931.

Hymns Ancient & Modern Revised. London: Hymns Ancient & Modern Ltd, 1972.

Hymns for Today's Church. London: Hodder and Stoughton, 1982.

The New English Hymnal. Norwich: The Canterbury Press Norwich, 1986.

Common Praise. Norwich: The Canterbury Press Norwich, 2000.

Ancient & Modern, Hymns and songs for refreshing worship. London: Hymns Ancient & Modern Ltd, 2013.

Online sources

This is a (far from comprehensive) summary of the many websites I have consulted during work on this book:

The Abbot's Leigh website: http://www.abbotsleigh.org.uk/index.html

AditNow: http://www.aditnow.co.uk/. A website devoted to the history of mining, with some useful information on the Great Western Colliery where the composer of CWM RHONDDA worked.

Archives Wales: http://www.archiveswales.org.uk/

BBC Gloucestershire Shnuggets:
http://www.bbc.co.uk/gloucestershire/content/articles/2009/01/05/midwinter_shnugget_feature.shtml. On the history of CRANHAM, most of which didn't make it into the book.

British History Online: https://www.british-history.ac.uk/. Contains a wealth of information about the early history of all sorts of 'little towns'.

The Canterbury Dictionary of Hymnology: http://www.hymnology.co.uk/. An invaluable resource for all sorts of hymn-related topics.

The Domesday Book Online: http://www.domesdaybook.co.uk/

Electric Scotland:
http://www.electricscotland.com/history/statistical/crimond.htm. My source for the original Gaelic name of Crimond.

Fionn Taylor's website: http://www.healeyhero.co.uk/rescue/menu.htm. Has some details about the 1893 disaster in the Great Western Colliery.

The Journal of the Folk-Song Society, No. 6, 1905. In which the prototypes of KINGSFOLD, MONKS GATE and FOREST GREEN were first published.

The Foreign & Commonwealth Office:
http://blogs.fco.gov.uk/ukincanada/2013/06/04/cecil-spring-rice-singing-the-unsung-hero/. Has some useful information on the author of *I vow to thee, my country*.

The Holst Birthplace Museum: http://www.holstmuseum.org.uk/index.htm. See especially the page about Holst's church music.

WORKS CONSULTED

Hymnary.org – a comprehensive index of hymns and hymnals: http://www.hymnary.org/

Mainly Norfolk: English Folk and Other Good Music: https://www.mainlynorfolk.info/folk/. Has some interesting background on KINGSFOLD, among others.

The Mudcat Café: http://mudcat.org/. Contains useful information about folksongs.

The Oxford Dictionary of National Biography (online edition): http://www.oxforddnb.com/public/index.html. This is a subscription service, but it is free if you have a library card.

The Ralph Vaughan Williams Society: http://www.rvwsociety.com/

The Rhondda Valleys website: http://www.rhonddavalleys.co.uk/index.htm

St James' Church Abinger Common: http://www.stjameschurchabinger.org/PN-apr01.ashx. For some information on ABINGER, RVW's tune for *I vow to thee, my country*.

Thaxted village website: http://www.thaxted.co.uk/

The Thaxted Morris Men: http://thaxtedmorris.org/

UK Censuses 1871 to 1911. These have proved especially useful for tracking down Henry Garman, Isaac and Frederick Longhurst, and Peter and Harriet Verrall. I accessed these via http://www.genesreunited.co.uk/

Welsh Coal Mines: http://www.welshcoalmines.co.uk/. Contains some historical information relevant to CWM RHONDDA.

Wikipedia: https://en.wikipedia.org/wiki/Main_Page. Love it or loathe it, Wikipedia is often a good place to start. It has the great virtue of nearly always quoting its sources, which can then be followed up and checked.

Books and articles

These are the printed sources I looked at; again, probably an incomplete list:

Telesforo Bini (ed), *Laudi Spirituali del Bianco da Siena, povero Gesuato del secolo XIV*. Lucca: G Giusti, 1851. The source of *Discendi amor santo (Come down, O Love divine)*.

Robert Bridges (ed), *The Spirit of Man, An Anthology in English & French from the Philosophers & Poets made by the Poet Laureate in 1915 & dedicated by gracious permission to His Majesty The King*. London: Longmans Green & Co, 1916. The book which brought William Blake's poem beginning *'And did those feet in ancient time...'* to a wider public.

Lucy Broadwood and J A Fuller Maitland, *English County Songs*. London: J B Cramer and Co, 1893. This is where KINGSFOLD earned its association with *Dives and Lazarus*.

The Foxearth and District Local History Society, *I Ring for the General Dance: Gustav Holst and Thaxted*, 2006

Peter Harvey, *Glory Laud and Honour*. London: Triangle, 1996. A discussion of the origins of some of the best-known hymns, mainly focusing on the words.

John Hawes, Christopher Kitching and Bryan Almond, *The Parish Church of St Mary the Virgin Primrose Hill—History and Guide*. London: The Friends of St Mary's Primrose Hill, 2009. Includes some information on Percy Dearmer, first Editor of *The English Hymnal*.

Simon Heffer, *Vaughan Williams*. London: Faber & Faber, 2000.

Imogen Holst, *Gustav Holst and Thaxted*. Originally published in the *Thaxted Bulletin*, 1974. Reprinted, with additional material, by Thaxted Parochial Church Council, 1994.

D Jardine ('A member of the Philadelphia Bar'), *Celebrated Trials of All Countries and Remarkable Cases of Criminal Jurisprudence*. Philadelphia: Jesper Harding, 1847. Contains a detailed account of the murder of Maria Marten and the capture and trial of William Corder.

Works Consulted

William Jennings Bryan, *Heart to heart appeals*. New York: Fleming H Revell Company, 1917. The book which spurred Cecil Spring-Rice to revise his poem and turn it into what we now know as *I vow to thee, my country*.

Ronald Johnson, *How far is it to Crimond?* Bulletin of the Hymn Society, 176, July 1988, pp. 38-42. A summary of the arguments over who composed CRIMOND.

Alan Luff (ed), *Strengthen for Service: 100 years of The English Hymnal 1906–2006*. Norwich: Canterbury Press Norwich, 2005.

Bernard S Massey, *Cyril Vincent Taylor 1907-91*. Bulletin of the Hymn Society 189, October 1991, pp. 69-71.

Jan Morris, *The Matter of Wales*. Penguin Books, 1986.

Julian Onderdonk, *Hymn Tunes from Folk-songs: Vaughan Williams and English Hymnody*, in *Vaughan Williams Essays*, edited by Byron Adams. Aldershot: Ashgate Publishing Company, 2003.

John Owen Ward (ed), *The Oxford Companion to Music (tenth edition)*. London: Oxford University Press, 1970.

Cecil Sharp, *English Folk-Carols*. London: Novello & Co, 1911.

Ursula Vaughan Williams, *RVW*. London: Oxford University Press, 1988. An insightful biography by the composer's second wife.

Tony Wales, *The West Sussex Village Book*. Newbury: Countryside Books, 1984. Includes an account of a meeting with the son of Harriet and Peter Verrall.

Marcus Weeks, *Sussex Music*. Alfriston: Snake River Press, 2008.

Andrew Wilson-Dickson, *The Story of Christian Music*. Oxford: Lion, 2003.

Fenton Wyness, *Spots from the Leopard (Stories of Aberdeen and the North-east)*. Aberdeen: Impulse Books, 1971. Notable for Chapter 42: *Who really composed* CRIMOND?

INDEX

Names of hymn-tunes are shown in SMALL CAPS. Titles of books, hymns, poems or other works are given in *italics*. Page references in **bold** indicate a substantial passage—either a whole chapter or a biographical panel.

A

A Blacksmith courted me, 128
A safe stronghold our God is still, 11
ABBOT'S LEIGH, 6, **75–81**
ABERDEEN, 6, 151
ABERYSTWYTH, 6, 147
ABINGER, 69
Abrahams, Harold, 42
Addison, Joseph, 149
AGINCOURT, 150
All people that on earth do dwell, 14
All things bright and beautiful, 5
ALL THINGS BRIGHT AND BEAUTIFUL, 5
Amazing Grace, 77
Amiel, François, 35
Angels from the realms of glory, 92
Anglican chant, 13
ANTIOCH, 150
Archduke Trio (Beethoven), 77
Areopagitica (Milton), 60
Arglwydd, arwain trwy'r anialwch, 91, 93, See also *Guide me, O thou great Jehovah*
Arne, Thomas, 46
At a Solemn Musick, 46
AUSTRIA, 77, 78, 151

B

Bach, Johann Sebastian, 32, 33, 35, 36
Ballad of Maria Martin, The, 108, 22, 115, 116, 118
BALLANTINE, 27
BANGOR, 6
Banks of Green Willow, The, 126
BATH, 151
Bax, Sir Arnold, 24
BBC Hymn-Book, The, 80
Be still, my soul: the Lord is on your side, 151
BEDFORD, 6, 18
Beethoven, Ludwig van, 77, 125
BELGRAVE, 6
BESANÇON, 150
BLACKBIRD LEYS, 148
BLAENWERN, 90, 147
Blake, William, 57, 58, 59; *Milton* (poem), 57–59
Blest Pair of Sirens, 46
Bonar, Horatius, 116, 118
BONN, 150
Book of Common Prayer, 11, 16
Booker, Mr, 108, 112, 115, 116, 118
Brave New World, 49
BRETBY, 43
Bridge, Frank, 44

Bridges, Robert, 32, **34**, 35, 36, 59, 60, 101; *The Spirit of Man*, 59; *The Yattendon Hymnal*, 34–36
Brind, Edward, 44
BRISTOL, 18
British Tars, The, 113
Broadwood, John, 125
Broadwood, Lucy, 68, 71, 119, 125, 141, 150; *English County Songs*, 119
Broadwood, Revd John, 141
Bromswick Tune (Hanover), 17
Brooks, Phillips, 137, 141, 142
Brother James's Air, 22
Brown, A H, 148
Bruch, Max, 98
Bryan, William Jennings, 69, 70
Bulletin of the Hymn Society, 26, 80
Bunyan, John, 129
Bushes and Briars, 108
Butterworth, George, **126**

C

Calvert, John, 86
Cân a Mawl, 92
Caniadau y rhai sydd ar y Môr o Wydr, 91
Canterbury Dictionary of Hymnology, 27
CARLISLE, 151
Carnie, William, 25, 27
CHARING CROSS, 43
Charles II, 75, 76
CHESHIRE, 16, 18
Chesterton, G K, 101
CHICHESTER, 18
Christ is made the sure foundation, 149
Christ is our corner-stone, 148
Christians awake, salute the happy dawn, 148
Christians lift up your hearts, 103
CHRISTMAS CAROL, 59, 138
Church Porch, The, 138
Clark, Thomasa, 149

Clarkson, Jeremy, 42
Cliffe, Charles, 85
Clubb, William, 26, 27
COE FEN, 148
Columbus, Christopher, 46
Come all ye faithful Christians, 113, 114, 118
Come down, O Love divine, 5, 103
Come, ye thankful people, come, 149
Common Measure. *See* Common Metre
Common Metre, 12
Common Praise, 27, 93
Congregational Hymns, 54
Conyers, Richard, 149
Cooper, Robert, 26
Corder, William, **109–11**, 111
CORNWALL, 151
Coverdale, Miles, 10, 15
CRANBROOK, 149
CRANHAM, 66, 148
Creek, Jonathan, 111
CRIMOND, **21–28**
Cromwell, Thomas, 41, 42
Cutts, Peter, 148
CWM RHONDDA, **85–93**

D

D'Urfey's Pills to Purge Melancholy, 114
Darwin, Caroline, 98
Darwin, Charles, 68, 98, 114
Darwin, Emma, 98
Davies, Richard, 88
Day's Psalter. See Whole Book of Psalms
Dear Lord and Father of mankind, 3, 48, 54; *The Brewing of Soma*, 50–53
Dearmer, Revd Percy, 35, 87, 100, **101**, 102, 116, 141; *He who would valiant be*, 131–33
Deutschland, Deutschland über alles, 79, *See also Lied der Deutschen*

INDEX

DEVONSHIRE, 151
Dictionary of National Biography, 44
Dingle, John, 114
Discendi, amor santo, 103
Dives and Lazarus, 119
Doane, G W, 24
Doddridge, Philip, 149
DOMINUS REGIT ME, 22
Doors of Perception, The, 49
Dowland, John, 15
DOWN AMPNEY, 5, **97–104**
DUKE STREET, 149
DUNDEE, 18, 151
DUNFERMLINE, 151
DURHAM, 18
Dykes, John Bacchus, 22, 117; DOMINUS REGIT ME, 22; MELITA, 150; NICAEA, 150; VOX DILECTI, 118
Dylan, Bob, 113

E

EASTER HYMN, 102
Edward VI, 10
Edward VIII. *See* Windsor, Duke of
Eight Traditional English Carols, 127
EIN' FESTE BURG, 11
Elgar, Sir Edward, 44, 59, 61
Elizabeth I, 10, 86
Elizabeth II, 23
Elvey, George, 149
England's Pleasant Land, 59
ENGLANDS LANE, 150
English County Songs (Broadwood & Fuller Maitland), 119
English Folk Dance and Song Society, 125
English Hymnal, The, 5, 35, 36, 87, 93, 101, 102, 103, 116, 117, 118, 119, 127, 132, 141, 147
English National Opera, 129
ESSEX, 151

Este, Thomas, 15, 17, 147
Eternal Father, strong to save, 117, 150
ETWALL, 43
Evans, Harry, 92
EVERTON, 151

F

FALKLAND, 5
FARLEY CASTLE, 5
FARMBOROUGH, 5
FARNABY, 5
FARNHAM, 5, 150
FARRANT, 5
Father, hear the prayer we offer, 127
Ferguson, William, 148
FFIGYSBREN, 5
Fight for Right, 60
Fight the good fight, 150
Filby, William Charles, 150
FINLANDIA, 151
FIRST MODE MELODY, 5
Fisher, Geoffrey, 42, 43
FITZWILLIAM, 5
FOLKINGHAM, 5
Folk-Song Society, 68
For all the saints (hymn), 3, 103
FOR ALL THE SAINTS (tune), 5
For the beauty of the earth, 150
FOREST GREEN, 5, **137–42**, 150
Francis II (Holy Roman Emperor), 77, 78
Fuller Maitland, John Alexander, 119, 125

G

Garden, Graeme, 42
Garman, Henry, 140, 141, 142
Geneva, 15
George VI, 24

Gerhardt, Paul, 36
GERONTIUS, 117
Gilderoy, 114, 115, 118, 119
Gladstone, William Ewart, 54
Gladstone, William Henry, 54, 150
Glasgow Orpheus Choir, 24
GLASSENBURY TUNE, 16
Glorious things of thee are spoken, 4, 5, 76, 77, 78, 79, 88
GLOUCESTER, 151
God be in my head, 59
God moves in a mysterious way, 149
God Save the Queen, 3, 59
Golden Pippin, The, 149
Goostly Psalms (Coverdale), 15
Goss, John, 5
Gott erhalte Franz den Kaiser, 78, 79
Grace, 'tis a charming sound, 149
Grant, David, 25, 26, 27; CRIMOND, **21–28**
Great Bible, 10, 11, 15
Griffiths, Ann, 92
Grimm, Wilhelm and Jacob (the Brothers Grimm), 31
Grove, George, 44
Grove's Dictionary of Music and Musicians, 44
Guide me, O thou great Jehovah/Redeemer, 91, 93

H

Hail the day that sees him rise, 147
Hail thee, festival day, 103
HAMMERSMITH, 54, 150
Handel, George Frideric, 150; *Solomon*, 46
HANOVER, 17, 150
Hark the herald angels sing, 17
Harris, Howell, 89, 91
Hatton, John, 149
Haweis, Thomas, 150

Haydn, Joseph, 4, 78
He who would valiant be, 3, 132–33
Heart to Heart Appeals, 70
HELMSLEY, 149
Henry VIII, 10, 15, 41, 88
Hensley, Everard, 139
HEREFORD, 151
Hesse, Johannes, 33
Hills of the north, rejoice, 148
Hoffmann, August Heinrich, 79
Holmes, Sherlock, 111
Holst, Adolph, 67
Holst, Clara, 148
Holst, Gustav, 44, 65, **66**, 71, 72; CRANHAM, 148; THAXTED, **65–72**; *The Planets*, 66
Holy, holy, holy, 117, 150
Hopkins, Gerald Manley, 34
Hopkins, John, 15, 18, *See also Whole Book of Psalms*
Horder, William Garett, 54
HORSHAM, 150
Houseman, A E, 126
How great thou art, 54
How shall I sing that majesty, 148
Hughes, John, **91**; CWM RHONDDA, **85–93**
Huntingdon, William R, 138
Hurn, Robert, 126
Huxley, Aldous, 49
HYFRYDOL, 90
Hymns Ancient & Modern, 18, 22, 35, 36, 42, 43, 78, 93, 100, 101, 117, 133
Hymns of Faith and Hope, 116

I

I heard the voice of Jesus say, 116, 117
I vow to thee, my country, 70, 72
I'm Sorry I Haven't a Clue, 3
In the bleak midwinter, 66, 148
INNSBRUCK, **31–36**, 150

Innsbruck, ich muss dich lassen, 32
Ireland, John, 44
Irvine, Anna Barbara, 26, 27
Irvine, Jessie Seymour, 26, 27;
   CRIMOND, **21–28**
Irvine, Revd Alexander, 26
Isaac, Heinrich, 32, 33, 35, 36;
   INNSBRUCK, **31–36**, 150

J

JERUSALEM, 43, **57–61**, 150
Jesu, lover of my soul, 147
Joseph of Arimathea, 58
Journal of the Folk-Song Society, 114, 115, 116, 119, 125, 127
Joy to the world, 150
Just as I am, 148

K

Kemp, Revd Dr, 27
KENT, 151
KENTISH TUNE, 16
Kethe, William, 15
KILMARNOCK, 151
KING'S LANGLEY, 150
KING'S LYNN, 150
KING'S WESTON, 150
KINGSFOLD, **107–18**, 150
Kipling, Rudyard, 34

L

Land of Hope and Glory, 59
Lane, Jane, 75
LASST UNS ERFREUEN, 102
Lay of the Last Minstrel, The (Scott), 60
Lied der Deutschen, Das, 79
Light's abode, celestial Salem, 149
LITTLE CORNARD, 148

Littledale, Richard Frederick, 103
LIVERPOOL, 151
LLANFAIR, 147
Llyfr y Psalmau, 88, 89
Lo! he comes with clouds descending, 149
LONDON, 149
LONDON NEW, 149
Long since in Egypt's plenteous land (Parry), 47–48
Longhurst, Frederick, 139
Longhurst, Isaac, 140, 142
Lord of all hopefulness, 148
LOURDES, 150
Love divine, all loves excelling, 147
Lusitania, RMS, 70
Luther, Martin, 11, 33
Lyall, Revd James E, 28

M

Magnificat, 9
Malkin, B H, 85
MANNHEIM, 150
Marten, Ann, 109, 110, 111
Marten, Maria, **109–11**
Marten, Thomas, 109, 110
Martin, H A, 43
Mary had a little lamb, 12
Mary I, 10, 41
Massey, Bernard, 80
Master and Commander, 113
Maximilian I (Holy Roman Emperor), 32
McCartney, Paul, 137
McCauley, Richard, 138
McEwan, John, 24
Medici, Lorenzo de', 32
MELITA, 117, 150
Mendelssohn Bartholdy, Felix, 46
Miller, Edward, 78
Milton, John, 46, 57, 60
Milton, John (composer), 129

MONKS GATE, 101, **123–34**, 150
Monteith, Revd Robert, 26
Morgan, William, 88
Morganwg, Iolo. *See* Williams, Edward
Morris, Jan, 85
Morrison, Jim, 49
MOSCOW, 150
My God, how wonderful thou art, 149
My old man's a dustman, 3

N

National Anthem. *See God Save the Queen*
National Union of Women's Suffrage Societies, 61
Naylor, Kenneth, 148
New English Hymnal, The, 27
Newton, John, 4, **77**, 79
NICAEA, 117, 150
Noble, John, 130
Noel, Conrad Le Dispenser, 68
NORTHAMPTON, 151
Northern Psalter, The, 25, 26
Northern Psalter, The, 27
Norton, George, 75, 76
Nun ruhen alle Wälder, 36
Nunc Dimittis, 9
NÜRNBERG, 150

O

O come all ye faithful, 4, 13
O God, our help in ages past, 12
O Jesus I have promised, 148
O little town of Bethlehem, 3, 59, 137, 138, 141
O Welt, ich muss dich lassen, 33
O worship the King, all glorious above, 17
O'Hara, Kane, 149
OLD HUNDREDTH, 15

Old Version, The. *See* Whole Book of Psalms
Olive, Leslie, 130
Olivers, Thomas, 149
On Christmas Night all Christians sing, 127
On Ilkla Moor baht 'at, 4, 149
On Jordan's bank the Baptist's cry, 149
Onward, Christian soldiers, 3, 4, 5
Origin of Species, The, 98
Our captain calls all hands, 127, 128, 133
Our Hymn Book, 131
Oxford Companion to Music, The, 102

P

Pange Lingua, 9
Paradise Lost, 57, 59
Parry, Joseph, 147
Parry, Sir Charles Hubert Hastings, 34, **43–45**, 54, 59, 60, 61, 66, 68, 98; JERUSALEM, 43, **31–36**, 150; *Judith* (oratorio), 45–48; REPTON, **41–54**; *The Music of the Seventeenth Century*, 45
Patrick, Revd Dr Millar, 26
Paxton Hood, E, 131
Pears, Revd J, 43
Pears, Steuart Adolphus, 42
Penfro Rowlands, Tom, 147
Penfro Rowlands, William, 147
People's Hymnal, The, 103
PETRA, 150
Philip, Duke of Edinburgh, 23
PICARDY, 150
Pilgrim's Progress, The, 129, 130
Ploughboy's Dream, The, 139–42
Poirot, Hercule, 111
Port, Sir John (c.1510–1557), 42
Port, Sir John (d.1540), 42
Pottipher, Mr, 108
PRAISE MY SOUL, 5, 24

INDEX

Praise the Lord, ye heavens adore him, 4, 78
Praise to the Holiest in the height, 117, 150
Praise, my soul, the King of Heaven, 5, 24
Prideaux, Humphrey, 46
Prys, Edmwnd, 88, 89
Psalm 100, 11, 12, 13; *All people that on earth do dwell*, 14
Psalm 23, 16; *The Lord's my shepherd*, 22; *The King of love my shepherd is*, 22; *The Lord is onely my support*, 16
Psalms, hymns and anthems for the Foundling Chapel, 78
Purcell, Henry, 149

R

RALEIGH, 26
Raleigh, Sir Walter, 26
Ramsey, Michael, 42
Rathbone, Basil, 42
Ravel, Maurice, 98
Ravenscroft, Thomas, 16, 22, 129, 147
Redhead, Richard, 150
Redner, Lewis, 137, 138
REGENT SQUARE, 149
REPTON, **41–54**, 61
REPTON SCHOOL, 43
Repton School Hymn-book, 42, 43, 61
RICHMOND, 150
Richmond, Revd Leigh, 150
Riddell, George, 27
RIEVAULX, 117
Riley, Athelstan, 102
Roberton, Hugh, 24
Rock of ages, 150
RODMELL, 150
Royal George, The, 125, 127
Rudolph, Archduke of Austria, 77
Rule, Britannia, 46, 59
RUSPER, 150

S

SAFFRON WALDEN, 148
Salesbury, William, 88
SALVE FESTA DIES, 103
SALZBURG, 150
Scholes, Percy, 102
Schumann, Robert, 137
Scopes Monkey Trial, 69
Scotsman, The, 26, 27
Scott of the Antarctic, 98
Scott, Sir Walter, 60
Scottish Psalter, 22
Sharp, Cecil, 68, 100, 108, 114, 125, 150
Shaw, Geoffrey, 150
Shaw, Martin, 148, 150
Sheeles, J, 149
Shepherds of the Delectable Mountains, The, 129
SHEPTON-BEAUCHAMP, 150
SHIPSTON, 150
Shropshire Lad, A, 126
Sibelius, Jean, 151
Siena, Bianco da, 103
Sine Nomine, 103, 104
SLANE, 148
Smart, Henry, 149
Songs of Praise (BBC programme), 54
Songs of Praise (hymn-book), 61, 69, 72
Songs of those upon the Sea of Glass, The. See Caniadau y rhai sydd ar y Môr o Wydr
SOUTHAMPTON, 151
Spring-Rice, Sir Cecil, 68, 69, 70; *The Two Fatherlands*, 70
St Ambrose, 9
St Augustine, 9
ST GEORGE'S WINDSOR, 149
ST GERTRUDE, 5
ST LOUIS, 138
St Matthew Passion, 33
St Paul, 150

St Petersburg, 150
Stalham, 150
Stanford, Charles Villiers, 66, 68, 98
Sternhold, Thomas, 15, 18, *See also* Whole Book of Psalms
Stockport, 148
Stocks, Dr George Gilbert, 43, 48, 54
Stravinsky, Igor, 137
Stuttgart, 150
Suffolk tune, 16
Summertown, 148
Surrey, 151
Sussex, 127, 151
Sussex Carol, 127
Sutton, Richard, 42

T

Taylor, Cyril Vincent, 4, **76**, 79; Abbot's Leigh, 6, **75–81**
Te Deum, 9
Temple, William, 42
Tennyson, Hallam (second Baron Tennyson), 125
Thacker, Gilbert, 41
Thacker, Thomas, 41
Thaxted, **65–72**
The King of love my shepherd is, 22
The Lord's my shepherd, 22, 23, 24
The spacious firmament on high, 149
There is a green hill far away, 3
Thomas, D W, 91
Tippett, Sir Michael, 66
To be a pilgrim. See *He who would valiant be*
Tolkien, J R R, 88
Turle, James, 149
Tyrol, 150

V

Vaughan Williams, Arthur, 97
Vaughan Williams, Margaret. *See* Wedgwood, Margaret
Vaughan Williams, Ralph, 35, 44, 61, 68, 71, **98**, 99, 102, 103, 107, 108, 115–18, 126, 128, 141, 142, 150, 151; Down Ampney, **97–104**; *Five Variants of Dives and Lazarus*, 119; Forest Green, 5, **137–42**, 150; Kingsfold, **107–18**, 150; *London Symphony*, 126; Monks Gate, **123–34**, 150; Salve Festa Dies, 103; Sine Nomine, 103; Sussex, 127; Sussex Carol, 127; *Symphony No. 5*, 129; *The Pilgrim's Progress*, 129–31; *The Ploughboy's Dream*, 139–42; *The Shepherds of the Delectable Mountains*, 129
Venice, 150
Verdi, 43
Verdi, Giuseppe, 43
Verrall, Frederick, 125
Verrall, Harriet, 124–25, 127
Verrall, Peter, 124–25, 126, 127
Vexilla Regis, 18
Victoria, Queen, 46
Vienna, 150
Voice from Galilee, The, 116
Vox Dilecti, 117, 118

W

Wainwright, John, 148
Walford Davies, Henry, 44, 59, 60, 138
War, 18
Watts, Isaac, 17
Webbe, Samuel, 150
Wedgwood, Emma. *See* Darwin, Emma
Wedgwood, Josiah I, 98

INDEX

Wedgwood, Josiah III, 98
Wedgwood, Margaret, 98
Wele'n sefyll rhwng y myrtwydd, 92
WELLS, 151
WENGEN, 138
Wesley, Charles, 17
Wesley, John, 17, 89, 149
Wesley, Samuel Sebastian, 44
WESSEX, 151
WESTMINSTER, 18, 149
Westminster Abbey, 23, 149
When I survey the wondrous cross, 17
Whicker, Alan, 107
While shepherds watched their flocks by night, 3, 4, 16, 22, 149
Whittier, John Greenleaf, 48, 50; *The Brewing of Soma*, 49, 50–53
Who would true valour see, 130–31, 131
Whole Book of Psalms, The (Sternhold & Hopkins), 15, 18, 88
WIGTON, 6
Williams Baker, Sir Henry, 22
Williams, Edward (Iolo Morganwg), 87, 88
Williams, Peter, 93
Williams, Robert, 147
Williams, Taliesin, 87

Williams, William (Pantycelyn), 90, **91**, 93
Wilson, President Woodrow, 70
WILTSHIRE, 151
WINCHESTER NEW, 149
WINCHESTER OLD, 16, 18, 22, 149
WINDERMERE, 151
WINDSOR, 18
Windsor, Duke of, 23
Winkworth, Catherine, 36
WOLVERCOTE, 148
Women's Institute, 61
Wood, Charles, 126
Wooldridge, Harry Ellis, 34, 35

Y

Yattendon Hymnal, The, 34, 35, 36
Ye watchers and ye holy ones, 102
Yesterday, 3
YORK, 129, 148
YORKSHIRE, 6, 148
You'll never walk alone, 3

Z

Zimmerman, Robert. *See* Dylan, Bob